UNITY, TRUST, CAMARADERIE:

NOW CAMP DEVOTIONS FOR YOUNG LIVES

**By Karen Fitzpatrick
Founder of NOW Ministries, Inc.**

Copyright Page

© 2021 Karen Fitzpatrick
**UNITY, TRUST, CAMARADERIE:
NOW Camp Devotions For Young Lives**

First Printing

All rights reserved. Reproduction in whole or part without written permission from the publisher or author is strictly prohibited. Printed in the United States of America.

All scripture is taken from the NIV version of the Bible unless otherwise specified.

Karen Fitzpatrick
Chesapeake, Virginia

Simply This Publishing
Kindle Direct Publishing

TABLE OF CONTENTS:

Dedication: Page 5

Introduction: Page 7

UNITY: Page 9

Unity With God: Pages 10 - 37

Unity With Others: Pages 38 - 65

TRUST: Page 66

Trust in God: Pages 67 - 93

Trusting Others: Pages 94 - 121

CAMARADERIE: Page 122

Camaraderie With God: Pages 123 - 149

Camaraderie With Others: Pages 150 - 177

Pastor Karen's Testimony: Page 178

How to Become a Christian: Pages 181 - 186

A Prayer to Receive Jesus: Page 187

Contact Information: Page 189

The Ten Commandments: Page 190

The Fruit of the Spirit: Page 191

Jesus Loves Me Lyrics: Page 192

Interesting Facts About the Bible: Page 193

About the Author: Page 194

DEDICATION

This book is dedicated to the glory of God, the Father, God, the Son and God, the Holy Spirit, the First, the Last, the Alpha and Omega.

It is next dedicated to my dear, dear mother, Judith Gail Chaffee Thomas who battled to raise a strong-willed child like me. There is no doubt in my mind that she is the one that God chose for the grueling task of confronting me when I was wrong, bringing consequences for my actions and standing firm in her convictions, no matter what life threw her way.

Through the years, my mother has become one of my heroes. The duty and bravery that she has displayed throughout her lifetime still amazes me and comforts me when I feel unskilled at navigating life's challenges. I often still hear her voice guiding me and telling me to, "Do what's right, because it's right!! Keep your commitments. Keep your word, even when it's hard and no one else is living that level of honesty." My mother showed me how to stand when others would not. My mother showed me what sacrifice looks like and that it sometimes costs you everything.

I will forever be grateful that my mother was a mother first before anything else. She made sure that her children were okay before she was. This set me up to see the sacrificial love, grace and mercy of Jesus Christ. I will forever be grateful for the family meals and memories forged because our home was a welcoming place. I will remember all the good times shared. I will remember the many times that my mother went without, so that others could have plenty and her love of people over things, objects and money.

I believe with all my heart that my mother, Judith Gail Chaffee Thomas was hand-picked by God for me. My mother, "Judism, Jude, Mamasita, Old Lady," you were born for me. You were my light in the darkness, even when we both fell prey to dark choices. Thank you, mom, for every good and perfect gift. Thank you for loving me by correcting me and telling me what I needed to hear, not what I wanted to hear. Thank you for telling me, "NO!"

Mom, you will forever be my voice of reason and special confidant. What you have taught me lives on in me and in my children and no doubt, in the generations to come.

Love,
Your Daughter,
Karen Fitzpatrick
May 2021

INTRODUCTION

In January of 2021, I was in our Wakefield, VA camp location praying in the sanctuary when the Lord spoke to my heart about the theme for this year's NOW Leadership Camp. He clearly spoke to me that this year's theme would be: UNITY, TRUST, CAMARADERIE! The Lord began to download activities and ideas to help share this message with the young people and workers who would attend our NOW Leadership Camp in July of 2021. It was then that the Lord showed me that I would also write a devotional book to sign and give to each young person in attendance at camp this year. At first, it seemed like an exciting task, however, then I started the actual writing and realized the commitment and prayer to complete this work would be more difficult than I thought, but with God's help, the book you have in your hands is the result of the vision God gave me back in January 2021. Each page is filled with a scripture, a message from me, a prayer and a declaration. All four parts of each page are important to complete if you are to grow strong in UNITY TRUST and CAMARADERIE with yourself, others and God. Take time everyday to read at least one writing and write in the margins if you want to. God may give you an insight or bring something important to your mind. Go ahead and make this devotional book your own. Use highlighters, too. All these tools are good practice in the study of God's Word.

My prayer is that these devotional exercises will help you to understand God and His kingdom better. That it will help you to understand just how important it is that the church learns how to get along and walk together in unity, but this takes trust in God and wisdom to walk in trust with others. It also takes a lot of mercy and forgiveness. We all make mistakes, and we need to hold one another accountable without breaking trust in God and unity with one another. We must learn to recognize how to deal with conflict and issues that arise. We also must learn when to walk away. Not all stories have a happy ending and sometimes it's best for people to part ways. Everything should be done from a place of love and should keep God's kingdom work in mind. It isn't always easy, but if we are to help the Lord Jesus to win souls for His kingdom, we need to get this. Unity produces peace and power. A unified church is a powerful church. May all of your endeavors for Jesus Christ be filled with His presence and power to walk in UNITY, TRUST and CAMARADERIE with yourself and with others in His Body, the Church.

In Christ Jesus,
Pastor Karen Fitzpatrick,
Founder and President of NOW Ministries, Inc.
May 2021

UNITY

"...until we all reach unity in the faith and in the knowledge of the Son of God and become mature, attaining to the whole measure of the fullness of Christ. (Ephesians 4:13)

UNITY WITH GOD

"My prayer is not for them alone. I pray also for those who will believe in me through their message, that all of them may be one, Father, just as you are in me and I am in you. May they also be in us so that the world may believe that you have sent me. (John 17:20,21)

NOTES

"For Yours is the kingdom and the power and the glory forever. Amen."
Matthew 6:13
(Number 1 of 4 for this scripture)

A KINGDOM IS A PLACE THAT IS USUALLY RULED BY A KING OR QUEEN.

In our scripture above we read the words, "For Yours is the kingdom." These words from the Bible are talking about God's kingdom which is made up of the heavens and the earth, or what the Bible calls, "The whole realm of His glory." The stars, the universe, the planets, the moon, the sun. These are all included in His kingdom with God as the King of it all. Afterall, God made it all, so doesn't He get to be in charge of it all? Of course He does! This means that no matter what, God will always have the final say in everything.

PRAYER:
Dear Heavenly Father,
Thank you for the sun, moon, and stars.
Thank you for the earth and for our eternal home in heaven.
Thank you that "YOURS" is the kingdom.
Thank you that I'm part of that kingdom.
Help me to know You more.
I pray this in your wonderful name, Jesus.
AMEN!

DECLARATION:
(say out loud 3 times)

I AM PART OF GOD'S KINGDOM

**"For Yours in the kingdom and the power and the glory forever. Amen."
Matthew 6:13
(Number 2 of 4 for this scripture)**

WHAT DOES GOD MEAN WHEN HE SAYS THAT HIS KINGDOM IS A KINGDOM OF POWER?

Electrical power is what turns on your lights. Lightning is power in the sky. The water that pours over Niagara Falls is powerful. The wind's power helps to generate energy to fuel the electricity in homes. The sun's power gives us light each day. The moon and star's power give us light each night, but God's power is behind all these things and when put all together, is much bigger and stronger than all of these put together. Your big brother may be strong enough to lift you over his head. He may have the power to do this. God is like this. He has the POWER to lift us. He has the power to help us. His power is strong, big and mighty. His power formed the planets, sun, moon and stars and His power formed you. His power set in motion all of Creation. The trees, the animals, the land, the seas and people. God uses His power to bring about good, while Satan uses his limited power to bring about evil. This is why there is bad in the world. People yield to Satan instead of God. God has given you His power too! He has given you the power to pray to Him, the power to help the sick, the power to do great things, but the greatest power He has given you is the power of CHOICE! If you will

CHOOSE to love His Son, Jesus, you will also be given the POWER to become a child of God and live forever in heaven. You must use your power to choose Jesus over the Devil.

PRAYER:
Dear Heavenly Father,
Thank you for your power.
Thank you for making all of Creation.
Thank you for making me.
Help me, Lord to be powerful like You.
Help me to use my power to choose good over evil in everything.
In Your precious name I pray.
AMEN!

DECLARATION:
(say out loud 3 times)

I AM POWERFUL FOR GOD

> "For Yours is the kingdom and the power and the glory forever. Amen."
> Matthew 6:13
> (Number 3 of 4 for this scripture)

IN THE DICTIONARY, THE WORD GLORY MEANS: HIGH RENOWN OR HONOR WON BY NOTABLE ACHIEVEMENTS, MAGNIFICENCE OR GREAT BEAUTY.

Maybe you have a notable achievement like an award for straight A's, or Good Citizenship. Maybe you have visited places of great beauty and majesty like the Grand Canyon or Rocky Mountains. Maybe you've seen a puppy be born or held a newborn baby in your arms. Maybe you've climbed the highest mountain or traveled across the deepest ocean. I tell you the truth, that all of these things are just a little picture of what God's glory is like. Nothing in this world can compare to His excellence, wonder and perfection. The Bible says that God is altogether wonderful, altogether beautiful. There is no one like Him. No one. God's glory is His excellence. Just think of when you do something really well at school, or at home and you receive praise from your teachers, or your mom and dad, aunt, or uncle. This is a little like God's glory, too. He has done so well in creating us and loving us and taking care of us. He has done so well in making a way for us to get to heaven through His Son Jesus Christ. He has done all things well, even when we don't understand and don't deserve it. He is an excellent

God and Father. A perfect Savior and Friend and He deserves all of our praise.

PRAYER:
Dear Heavenly Father,
Thank you for your glory.
Thank you that you're an excellent God.
Thank you that you are wonderful and majestic and glorious.
Thank you for sending Jesus to die for me.
Help me to give you all the praise forever and ever.
AMEN!

DECLARATION:
(say out loud 3 times)

I SERVE AN EXCELLENT GOD

"For Yours is the kingdom and the power and the glory forever. Amen."
Matthew 6:13
(Number 4 of 4 for this scripture)

DID YOU KNOW THAT GOD HAS NO BIRTHDAY?

That's right! God wasn't born from a mother like you and me. He's always been around, and His kingdom will never end. You and I are part of His kingdom and because of Jesus; we can live with God in heaven forever and ever and ever. We will see our families and friends there. We will live there in peace with no more sickness and no more dying. It will be wonderful. Believe in Jesus. He is the way to this eternal, forever home and make sure to tell others about Jesus too so that they will live forever in heaven with God and with us.

PRAYER:
Dear Heavenly Father,
Thank you that you are the kingdom and the power
and the glory forever.
Thank you that I can trust You and your Son, Jesus to
lead me to heaven.
Help me Lord to trust you more and more each day.
It is in Your name that I pray.
AMEN!

DECLARATION:
(say out loud 3 times)

I WILL LIVE FOREVER IN HEAVEN WITH JESUS

> **"But seek first the kingdom of God and His righteousness, and all these things shall be added to you."**
> **Matthew 6:33**

WHEN YOU PLAY A VIDEO GAME, OR A BOARD GAME, YOU MUST LEARN THE RULES TO PLAY.

In order to win, you must play skillfully and practice over and over to get better at the game you are playing. Everything works this way and God's kingdom is like this, too. In order to get bonus points and move to different levels or advance around the board of any popular board game, or get better at ballet, or playing an instrument, you must follow the directions and do your best. When you do your best, you have a higher chance of winning. God's video game, or board game is the Bible and when we are faithful to do what it says, God will give us more. When we learn to do more and more of what the Bible expects, more help is given to us. Things like more love, more joy, more peace, more understanding and even when we make mistakes and break God's rules, we get a do over every time if we tell God we're sorry. Jesus is our "Get out of jail free" card, or our extra points to boost us to the next level in our video game. His death on the cross makes it so we can be forgiven and start again every time we need to. No game on earth can do that.

PRAYER:
Dear Heavenly Father,
Forgive me for not doing things Your way.
Help me to study Your word
Live Your word
And keep Your word.
In Jesus' name.
AMEN!

DECLARATION:
(say out loud 3 times)

I DO WHAT IS RIGHT EVEN WHEN IT'S HARD

"We love Him, because he first loved us."
1 John 4:19

WHEN WE WERE LITTLE BABIES, WE RELIED ON OUR PARENTS OR CAREGIVERS FOR EVERYTHING.

They fed us, changed our diapers, put us to bed, played with us, bought us presents, took us to school, read to us, celebrated birthdays with us, took us on vacations and took care of us when we were sick. Over time, we learned to love and trust our parents, or caregivers, too because they showed us love before we could even understand what love is. God is like this. Before we're able to understand what His Son, Jesus did on the cross for us, He walks beside us and whispers to us, "Jesus, My Son died for you! Believe in Him and I will grant you eternal life."

PRAYER:
Thank you Heavenly Father for Your Son, Jesus.
Thank you, Lord that I love You because You first loved me.
Forgive me, Lord Jesus when I take Your love for granted.
Help me, Lord to love You more and more each day.
In Jesus' name I pray.
AMEN!

DECLARATION:
(say out loud 3 times)

I LOVE JESUS BECAUSE HE FIRST LOVED ME

> **"Jesus said to him, "I am the way, and the truth, and the life; no one comes to the Father but through Me."**
> **John 14:6**
> **(1 of 3 for this scripture)**

"JESUS SAID TO HIM, "I AM THE WAY..."

WHEN MY CHILDREN WERE YOUNGER WE TOOK THEM TO A GIANT HAY MAZE.

They had so much fun trying to find "THE WAY" out. They tried this way and that way, but there was ONLY ONE WAY OUT and they all needed our help to find it. They would walk and walk and be fine for a while, but then they'd eventually get lost and call out for my husband or myself to come help them find the right way again. Sometimes it was hard to determine which way to go, but the right way always presented itself and we were able to continue. The hay maze reminds me of when Jesus told his disciples that He was the only WAY to the Father, our God in heaven and just like in that hay maze, as long as we followed the right way, we found our way out. The world will tell you that you can get to our Father, God in heaven by being a good person or saying your prayers or going to church, but these things are NOT THE WAY to the Father in heaven. Jesus said, "I AM THE WAY." So, trust in Jesus! Follow His teachings, do what they say and He will lead you in His WAY all your life, everyday and all the WAY TO HEAVEN.

PRAYER:
Dear Father in heaven,
Thank you for Jesus.
Thank you that He is the WAY to get to You.
He is the WAY to You and to my eternal home in heaven.
Please help me Lord to follow Jesus all my life and when
I get lost, help me find my way to Jesus again, just like in the hay maze.
I ask these things in Jesus' name.
AMEN!

DECLARATION:
(say out loud 3 times)

JESUS IS THE WAY

"Jesus said unto him, "I am the way, and the truth, and the life; no one comes to the Father but through me."
John 14:6
(2 of 3 for this scripture)

"AND THE TRUTH..."

HAVE YOU EVER HAD SOMEONE LIE TO YOU, OR JUST CHANGE THEIR MIND ABOUT SOMETHING?

Maybe they told you you'd get something for Christmas and then they forgot. Maybe a friend promised to call you, or come over, but they forgot. Maybe you were told that you would be going on a special trip, but the person changed their mind. Or, maybe someone told you something that turned out to be a lie! Jesus is not like this. In fact, Jesus told His disciples that He was the TRUTH! What does this mean? It means that there is no darkness in him. It means that you can trust Him and He never lies. It means that you can trust the Bible and you can trust that Jesus and His Word, the Bible, will never change. Jesus and His Word are the same yesterday, today and forever. Everything written in the Bible about Jesus is the truth and He is the Son of God. He is who He said He was. He is truthful and never lies. He is the One, True God! He is the truth!

PRAYER:
Dearest Lord and Savior,
Thank you for the truth in the Bible.
Thank you that You are the truth and the way to the Father in heaven.
Thank you that living your way will guide us into all truth in Your Word.
Thank you that you never lie and there is no darkness in You.
Help me to live for truth.
Help me to live your way dear Lord.
In Your name I pray this.
AMEN!

DECLARATION:
(say out loud 3 times)

JESUS IS THE TRUTH

> **"Jesus said to him, "I am the way, and the truth, and the life; no one comes to the Father but by me."**
> **John 4:16**
> **(3 of 3 for this scripture)**

"AND THE LIFE..."

HAVE YOU EVER DONE SOMETHING THAT YOU SHOULDN'T HAVE DONE?

How did it make you feel? Did you get in trouble for what you did? Did you do it again? Chances are that the more you do wrong, the harder things become. You may lose friends, or make your parents feel they can't trust you anymore. If you continue to do wrong, you could be expelled from school, or even worse. When we do things we shouldn't, God calls it sin. Sin entered the world through the first man, Adam and the first woman, Eve. They disobeyed God and would have been eternally separated from Him if it weren't for Jesus' sacrifice on the cross for our sins. When we put our trust in what Jesus did for us, it's like we cross over from death to life. Jesus is like our bridge of protection from the rapid current of a mighty river in a barren wasteland. He sees us over the bridge and to safety on the other side where there is life and life more abundantly.

PRAYER:
Heavenly Father,
Thank you for the cross.
Thank you for dying for our sins.
Thank you that You are the Way, the Truth and the Life.
I trust in You completely.
AMEN!

DECLARATION:
(say out loud 3 times)

JESUS IS THE LIFE

> **"For God so loved the world that he gave his one and only Son, that whoever believes in him shall not perish but have eternal life."**
> **John 3:16**

THERE ARE MANY RELIGIONS IN THE WORLD, BUT ONLY ONE JESUS!

God loved us so much that He sent His only Son, Jesus into the world to be born, grow up and then die on a cross for our sins. Sins are things we do that break God's laws. Three days after Jesus died on the cross, He rose from the dead and then ascended (went up) into the clouds all the way to Heaven where He is seated at the right hand of God, the Father. Jesus is what makes Christianity different from other religions. Other religions teach that we can work our way to Heaven, or come back again as something, or someone else to work out our salvation over and over again till we get it right, but the Bible does NOT teach this. We are saved by the grace of God through faith in Jesus. God sent Jesus to pay the price for your sins and the sins of the whole world and when we believe and trust in what Jesus has already done for us, we gain eternal life. This means that when we die, we will go to be with Jesus and all believers in Heaven. Trust Jesus with your life on Earth and trust in what He did on the cross!

PRAYER:
Dearest Lord and Savior,
Thank you for saving me from my sins.
Thank you that when I trust in what you did on the cross,
I can have eternal life.
Help me Lord, to trust in what you did for me
And help me to tell others about it too.
In Jesus' name.
AMEN!

DECLARATION:
(say out loud 3 times)

I TRUST IN JESUS

**"Jesus replied, 'Very truly I tell you, no one can see the kingdom of God unless they are born again."
John 3:3**

HAVE YOU EVER SEEN PICTURES OF YOURSELF RIGHT AFTER YOU WERE BORN?

Maybe you were born in a hospital, or at home. Maybe you were born in another country or on the fourth of July. Wherever, or whenever you were born, more than likely, someone was holding you wrapped tightly in a little blanket and just like you were born into this world with skin and bones and a tiny body, there is another part of you called your spirit that needs to be born too. When Adam and Eve sinned and broke God's law in the Garden of Eden way back when time first began, they had bodies and spirits too that were not supposed to die, but their sin caused things to change. Because of Adam and Eve, we are all born with original sin and it has to be taken care of by asking Jesus to forgive us and become the Lord of our lives. We must make a choice to follow Jesus and trust what He did on the cross. This is why Jesus said in John chapter three that we all need to be, "born again." Someday we will be given new bodies that will never die, but until then, everyone's bodies will die, but our spirits don't have to when we trust in Jesus. Is YOUR spirit born again? If you're not sure, just ask Jesus to come alive in your spirit today. Ask Him to be born again in you today like He once was in Adam and

Eve. Tell Him you're sorry for breaking His laws in the Bible and that you want Him to help you learn to live His way. Ask Him today! Don't wait. Today is the day. Now is the time. Ask Him!

PRAYER:
Dearest Lord and Savior,
Thank you for saving me.
I want You to be the Lord of my life.
I want to live Your way.
I want You to be born again in me.
I want to read and study the Bible and go to church.
I want to grow and come to know You better.
In Jesus name.
AMEN!

DECLARATION:
(say out loud 3 times)

I AM BORN AGAIN IN JESUS

> **"...and all are justified freely by his grace through the redemption that came by Christ Jesus."**
> **Romans 3:24**

DID YOU EVER PLAY ANY POPULAR BOARD GAMES?

Chances are you have and chances are you know that there is a space on the board that you can land on called, "JAIL." Now, in order for you to continue to proceed around the board and "get out of jail," you must throw doubles on any of your next three turns, pay a $50 fine before you roll the dice on either of your next two turns, use your "GET OUT OF JAIL FREE" card, or buy this card from another player for a designated amount and use it to move when it is your turn. Romans 3:24 is like this. It explains the rules for getting out of spiritual jail. Putting our faith in Jesus Christ and what He did on the cross, is what "justifies" us, or makes us right again in God's eyes. Our trust in Jesus is our "GET OUT OF JAIL FREE" card. When we trust in his grace, or free gift that we really don't deserve, we are let go from sin and sins penalty which is eternal separation from God. This free gift of eternal life starts working the minute we whisper, "I trust You, Jesus." The world has a game called, SIN, but we have a much better game called, REDEMPTION. This is the game of putting your trust in Jesus to save you and heal you from all your wrongdoing, but just like any game, we must follow the rules to eventually win. Follow Jesus' rules in the Bible and you will win every day knowing that you are serving and loving Him and others.

PRAYER:
Dear Heavenly Father,
Thank you for being my "GET OUT OF JAIL FREE" card.
Thank you, that because I put my trust in You, I have Your free gift of eternal life.
Thank you for Your grace, Lord even though I don't deserve it, but because of Your sacrifice on the cross, I can have eternal life.
Thank you for "justifying" me and making me right again because of what
Jesus did on the cross.
When I make mistakes Lord, thank you that I can ask you to forgive me and try again.
Help me never to take this free gift of eternal life for granted and help me to tell others all about it.
I pray in your name, Lord Jesus.
AMEN!

DECLARATION:
(say out loud 3 times)

I AM RIGHT WITH GOD THROUGH FAITH IN JESUS

> "But if serving the Lord seems undesirable to you, then choose for yourselves this day whom you will serve...But as for me and my household, we will serve the Lord." Joshua 24:15

JOSHUA WAS THE GUY WHO TOOK OVER FOR MOSES AFTER MOSES DIED AND JOSHUA CHALLENGED THE PEOPLE OF GOD TO THINK CAREFULLY ABOUT WHO THEY WOULD SERVE.

In Joshua's day, the people would worship foreign Gods and idols, or statues made out of wood that someone carved, or designed. This sounds silly to us in our day and age, but we have our foreign Gods and idols too. Think about it. Whatever you place higher than God, whatever you give your time to more than God can become what you worship. God wants first place in our hearts. He doesn't want any place, but first place in our lives. He is God. He made us and loves us and sent His Son, Jesus to die for us on the cross. He wants us to come to Him first for everything. Let's have a look at some of the things that people go to fill their time or make them feel better. Things like sports, food, drugs, alcohol, sex, hobbies, people, and education, just to name a few. Anything that we use to make us feel better instead of going to God and letting Him heal us, is an idol. God wants and deserves FIRST PLACE. Biblically speaking, God should be first in all of our activities and relationships. If we will make Him first, all the rest of our lives will fall into place. Let Jesus be the center of everything. CHOOSE to serve Him every day of your life!

PRAYER:
Father,
Please forgive me
When I've put other people,
Or other things before You.
Help me to know You more.
Help me to put You FIRST
In all I say and do.
Through Jesus' name I pray,
AMEN!

DECLARATION:
(say out loud 3 times)

JESUS HAS FIRST PLACE IN MY LIFE

UNITY WITH OTHERS

"Make every effort to keep the unity of the Spirit through the bond of peace. There is one body and one Spirit, just as you were called to one hope when you were called; one Lord, one faith, one baptism; one God and Father of all, who is over all and through all and in all."

Ephesians 4:3-6

NOTES

> "Just as a body, though one, has many parts, but all its many parts form one body, so it is with Christ. For we were all baptized by one Spirit so as to form one body."
> 1 Corinthians 12:12, 13a

HAVE YOU EVER SEEN ONE OF THOSE SKELETONS HANGING IN YOUR SCIENCE CLASS AT YOUR SCHOOL, OR HOMESCHOOL CLASSROOM?

Did you know that the human skeleton has 206 bones total and that means you, too? That's right! You have 206 bones in your body right now that help you move and walk around; 206 bones to support your organs on the inside and your skin (your largest organ) on the outside. Even more amazing is that when you were born, you had about 300 bones that eventually fused (grew together) to form the 206 bones that you have now. Isn't that amazing? Just imagine if all those bones in our body didn't work together, or some were broken or missing. We would probably be in some pain and maybe even not be able to walk around, kick a ball, hold a pencil, or run around the soccer field. The bones have to do their part TOGETHER so that the whole body can function. Well, the family of God is like this too. In the scripture above, we read that Jesus' body, the Church is ONE, but has many parts, just like the skeleton is one, but has many parts. If you believe in Jesus, you are part of His Body, the Church and His Church is ALL OVER THE WORLD. God expects us, as His Body, to work together so that the world can see ONE BODY with all it's parts in working order. Like going to the doctor to keep your bones healthy, we go to the Lord in prayer and study the Bible to learn how to stay healthy towards other people in our Churches and in the Body of Christ all over the world.

PRAYER:
Dear Lord,
Thank you that Your Church all over the world
Is my family. Thank you that Your Church
Helps to tell others about You. Please help Your Body, the Church
To remain strong and working together all over the world.
In Jesus' name I pray.
AMEN!

DECLARATION:
(say out loud 3 times)

I AM PART OF THE BODY OF CHRIST

> **"How good and pleasant it is when God's people live together in unity!"**
> **Psalm 133:1**

I REMEMBER THE FIRST TIME I EVER SPONSORED AN OVERNIGHT CHRISTIAN SUMMER CAMP FOR KIDS.

At first, it seemed like some of the kids didn't really want to be there, especially the new kids who had no prior camp experience. I can still picture those first few days of camp. The kids argued with one another and complained about not having their cell phones, even though all around them were beautiful trees, blue skies, summertime fun and kids just like them who were experiencing all the same things they were feeling. Then something started happening. They started working together, playing together and laughing together. They started learning how to work with the other kids on their team and have fun while doing it. Pretty soon, they were all in it together. It was glorious to watch God bring those kids together and teach them how to love each other, so much so, that the girls dorm campers cried when they had to leave each other at the end of the week. Some of these same girls are still friends today and keep in touch with one another. The boys, too. At the end of the day, God's Word is so true, as we all experienced at camp. It truly is SO good and pleasant when His people live together in unity! Be a unity builder. Bring people together for Jesus!

PRAYER:
Dear Heavenly Father,
Thank you that we get to be a part of Your Family,
The Body of Christ, the Church.
Thank you that You love us and want us to love You by loving
One another in Christ Jesus.
Please help us to walk together in unity
With our fellow Christian brothers and sisters.
In Your Holy name we pray.
AMEN!

DECLARATION:
(say out loud three times)

I LIVE IN UNITY WITH OTHERS

> **"Though one may be overpowered, two can defend themselves. A cord of three strands is not quickly broken." Ecclesiastes 4:12**

HAVE YOU EVER SEEN ONE OF THOSE REALLY THICK ROPES WITH THREE PARTS TO IT?

Just imagine a regular skinny rope that suddenly has two more ropes wrapped around it. Suddenly, the skinny rope is three times thicker and stronger than before. This is what we as Christians are like. When we come together in love by going to church together, reading our Bibles together, praying together and helping each other, we are stronger than before. It's like going from a skinny rope to a big, thick, strong rope that can carry more and won't break easily. When you are a Christian and walking with others who love Jesus, too, you can know that someone will always have your back. Someone will always be looking out for you. We are stronger together!

PRAYER:
Dear Lord,
Thank you that we are stronger together.
Please help us to take care of one another.
Please help us to be like this three
Stranded cord of rope that You talk about
In Ecclesiastes 4:12.
In Jesus' name.
AMEN!

DECLARATION:
(say out loud 3 times)

WE ARE STRONG TOGETHER

> **"I appeal to you, brothers and sisters, in the name of our Lord Jesus Christ, that all of you agree with one another in what you say and that there be no divisions among you, but that you be perfectly united in mind and thought."**
> **1 Corinthians 1:10**

DO YOU EVER FIGHT WITH YOUR BROTHERS OR SISTERS?

If you're an only child, maybe you have had disagreements with your parents, or cousins, or your dog, or cat? The point is, people fight sometimes, but God wants us all to get along, especially with our brothers and sisters in Christ. That's right. Everyone that is a believer in Jesus is part of your family. Believers in Jesus are to love one another, help each other and get along with each other because Jesus wants us to and because we are ALL in the family of God together. This means that believers all over the world are related to you because of Jesus. How cool is that? Pretty cool indeed.

PRAYER:
Dear Lord,
Thank you that I am never alone.
Thank you that You are with me
And I also have brothers and sisters all over the world.
Please help me to get along with others,
Especially those who are in the Family of God.
Help me to serve others in my church and love them like You do.
In Jesus' name.
AMEN!

DECLARATION:
(say out loud 3 times)

I GET ALONG WITH OTHERS

> **"All the believers were one in heart and mind. No one claimed that any of their possessions was their own, but they shared everything they had."**
> **Acts 4:32**

THE EARLY CHURCH WAS A SPECIAL PLACE.

When the church first started after Jesus went up into Heaven, people met in each other's homes. They had everything in common and worked hard to take care of each other. They didn't demand their own way. They tried to take the things that Jesus had taught them and put them into practice. They even shared everything, especially with those who didn't have as much. Do you like to share? Do you try and take care of others in your church family and at home? If you do, then you are doing what the Lord wants you to do. If not, let's pray and ask the Lord to help you.

PRAYER:
Dearest Lord,
Thank you for all the believers all over the world.
Thank you for the church.
Thank you that we, Your people are the church.
Please help me to be like the early church.
Help me to do for others
And to share whatever I can
So that others can feel Your love and protection.
Please help Your church, Your people all over the world
To love You more and to love each other more and more each day.
In Jesus' name.
AMEN!

DECLARATION:
(say out loud 3 times)

I LOVE GOD AND HIS PEOPLE

> **"Whatever happens, conduct yourselves in a manner worthy of the gospel of Christ. Then, whether I come and see you or only hear about you in my absence, I will know that you stand firm in the one Spirit, striving together as one for the faith of the gospel."**
> **Philippians 1:27**

HAVE YOU EVER HEARD THE SAYING, "AGREE TO DISAGREE?"

This means that when you disagree with someone, rather than fight about it and demand your own way, form a truce and agree to just let things go. This can be a very good way to deal with your differences with other people because no one can agree on everything 100% of the time. Christians are no different, they will sometimes disagree. The key when in a disagreement is forgiveness and keeping the peace, harmony and unity with others. It's important to learn to work out your differences with others in a peaceful, loving way. This may mean talking about it with the person privately, or just letting it go, or maybe a meeting with your pastor would be in order. Whatever you decide, do your best every day to live in peace with others, especially those in your church.

PRAYER:
Dear Lord,
Thank you for a spiritual family.
Thank you for the church.
Thank you that I can come to You and pray.
Please help me to live in peace with others,
Especially those in the Family of God.
I pray for unity in Your church throughout the world.
In Your name I pray.
AMEN!

DECLARATION:
(say out loud 3 times)

I LIVE IN PEACE WITH OTHERS

> **"At the same time, God's hand was on the people in the land of Judah, giving them all one heart to obey the orders of the king and his officials, who were following the word of the Lord."**
> **2 Chronicles 30:12**

WHAT ABOUT PEOPLE IN AUTHORITY?

A person in authority is a police officer, pastor, dad, mom, teacher, king, president, boss, judge, etc. A person in authority is someone who is in charge of other people. Sometimes people in authority are not following God and they are doing things that are not right. This usually results in suffering and hardship for those working with them. The leader who does this, loses respect and the people working with them lose trust in them often resulting in people leaving, or complaining, or both. However, when a person in authority follows the Lord and tries to do what is right, the opposite can happen. People begin to come together and work for the Lord and for one another. The Lord will bless those in authority when they do what is right. The outcome will be happy, unified people coming together. Pray for your leaders. Pray they be godly, loving, honest and kind. Pray that you become this type of leader, too.

PRAYER:
Dearest Lord,
Thank you for leaders in the church.
Thank you for leaders in my school.
Thank you for leaders in my town, state and country.
Thank you for the leaders in my family.
Thank you that I can be a great leader too if I follow You.
Help me Lord, to do this. To follow You all of my life.
Help me to be a great leader like You
And help all of the leaders over me to love You
And to lead others according to Your Word.
In Jesus' name.
AMEN!

DECLARATION:
(say out loud 3 times)

I OBEY MY LEADERS

> "I urge, then, first of all, that petitions, prayers, intercession and thanksgiving be made for all people - for kings and all those in authority, that we may live peaceful and quiet lives in all godliness and holiness. This is good, and pleases God our Savior, who wants all people to be saved and to come to a knowledge of the truth."
> 1 Timothy 2:1-4

PEOPLE ARE PRECIOUS TO GOD; EVEN THE ONES YOU DON'T LIKE!

Instead of talking about people behind their back, instead of gossiping and demanding your own way, God wants you to pray for others, especially those in leadership like kings, presidents, moms, dads, police officers, fire fighters, teachers, pastors, church leaders, etc. When you pray for your leaders and give thanks for them, God promises that your lives will be better off. God wants you to pray for all people, especially those in leadership because it isn't easy to be a leader. There are many hardships and temptations, but when your leaders succeed, your lives are better overall. So, don't forget to pray for everyone you can, especially those in leadership.

PRAYER:
Dear Lord,
Thank you for the many leaders in my life.
Help me to pray for them, even the ones I don't always like.
Help me to be a great leader like You, Lord.
Help me to be kind, gentle and full of grace and mercy.
Just like you, Lord.
I ask these things in Your precious, holy name.
AMEN!

DECLARATION:
(say out loud 3 times)

I PRAY FOR MY LEADERS

> **"The man said, 'This is now bone of my bones and flesh of my flesh; she shall be called 'woman,' for she was taken out of man."**
> **Genesis 2:23**

IF YOU REALLY WANT TO UNDERSTAND SOMETHING, YOU NEED TO GO BACK TO THE BEGINNING.

In the beginning, God's world was perfect. There wasn't sin, or death, or sickness and everything was in perfect unity. Adam and Eve were in perfect harmony too, in fact, Eve was made from a rib that was taken from Adam's rib cage. God had Adam fall into a deep sleep and then took the rib from him that made Eve. Adam was so happy and so was Eve. They were ONE and they are a picture of how God wants husbands and wives to be. Unified in all their choices and decisions. When we are in unity with our spouse, our friends, our family, or others, it is a beautiful thing, and everything works as it should. It wasn't until Adam and Eve sinned that their perfect union with God and with each other was destroyed. Thankfully, God made a way for us to have unity with God and with others again when we put our faith in His Son, Jesus Christ. If you need peace in your relationships, ask Jesus to help you live for Him and to love others like you would love yourself. With God's help, we can learn to live in unity with others, even when we don't agree on things.

PRAYER:
Dear God,
I'm so sorry when I don't get along with others.
I'm sorry when people are not unified for You.
Please help me, Lord.
Please help Your people to learn to
Be unified with You and with each other.
In Your name I pray,
AMEN!

DECLARATION:
(say out loud 3 times)

I LIVE IN UNITY WITH GOD AND WITH OTHERS

> "When the woman saw that the fruit of the tree was good for food and pleasing to the eye, and also desirable for gaining wisdom, she took some and ate it. She also gave some to her husband, who was with her, and he ate it. Then the eyes of both of them were opened..."
> **Genesis 3:6,7a**

GOD TOLD ADAM AND EVE NOT TO EAT FROM THE TREE THAT WAS IN THE MIDDLE OF THE GARDEN OF EDEN WHERE THEY LIVED.

God also told them that they could eat from ANY OTHER TREE they wanted in the entire Garden of Eden. We see in these scriptures that Adam and Eve did not listen to God, but instead, listened to the voice of Satan speaking to them through a serpent. Satan knew that if he could get them to sin against God's Word to them, he could destroy the beautiful unity they had with God and each other. That's what Satan does. He tries to get us to disobey what the Word of God in the Bible tells us. Notice how the tree that was forbidden to them was found in the CENTER, or MIDDLE of the Garden. This is because God should be in the middle of all that we do and say. In fact, God told Adam and Even that they weren't even supposed TO TOUCH that tree at all. Why? Because we are to have NOTHING to do with sin! Be careful and make choices that give God the CENTER of your heart and life. Sin ruins your unity with God and with others.

PRAYER:
Dearest Lord,
Please help me to obey Your voice.
Help me to obey Your Word, the Holy Bible.
Help me to learn to do life Your way.
Help me to learn repentance so that
When I make a mistake, I come to You
Right away to say I'm sorry.
In Jesus' name,
AMEN!

DECLARATION:
(say out loud 3 times)

I WILL OBEY GOD'S WORD

> "The man said, 'The woman you put here with me - she gave me some fruit from the tree, and I ate it."
> **Genesis 3:12**

GOD DOESN'T WANT US TO BLAME OTHERS FOR OUR MISTAKES.

In the verse above, Adam blames Eve for what happened. A few passages later, Eve blames the Serpent, but the truth is, we ALL MUST CHOOSE TO DO WHAT IS RIGHT no matter what. God will hold us responsible for our own choices. If you go and read chapter three in the book of Genesis in the Bible, you will see that not only do Adam and Eve not take responsibility for what they did, but severe consequences were given to both Adam and Eve and their unity was broken with each other and with God. They were asked to leave the Garden and never return. This may seem harsh, but God knows what happens to us when we disobey His Laws and don't keep Him in the CENTER of our hearts and lives. We end up just like Adam and Eve unless we trust in Jesus to fix it all. Thank God we can turn to Christ to help us to obey and walk in unity with God and with others. When you mess up, just say your sorry and take responsibility for whatever you did. This will help to keep unity with God and unity with others.

PRAYER:
Dear Lord,
Thank you for the example of Adam and Eve.
I know that we all miss it sometimes,
But we can come to You and ask for forgiveness.
We can come to You and ask You to help us
To take responsibility for our actions.
Thank You, Lord.
In Jesus' name,
AMEN!

DECLARATION:
(say out loud 3 times)

I WILL NOT BLAME OTHERS FOR MY CHOICES

"Children, obey your parents in the Lord, for this is right. Honor your father and mother - which is the first commandment with a promise - so that it may go well with you and that you may enjoy long life on the earth."
Ephesians 6:1-3

NO MATTER HOW OLD YOU GET, THE LORD WANTS YOU TO HONOR YOUR MOTHER AND FATHER.

Honoring our parents is the 5th of the 10 Commandments God gave us to live by. It is also the first commandment with a promise attached to it. Honoring your mom and dad brings longer life. Now, sometimes we disagree with our parents, or maybe we aren't in a place where our relationship with our mother and father is exactly the way we think it should be. Even so, we are to honor our parents and those in leadership. This means that you find ways to agree to disagree. If you are in a tough spot, talk to a trusted adult, pastor, church leader, or friend, but whatever the case may be, God wants us to walk in honor and unity with our moms and dads, as much as possible. What does "honor" look like? It means not interrupting your parents when they are speaking. It means following their rules. It means discussing things quietly and calmly when you are feeling frustrated. It means helping your parents with chores and doing everything without arguing and complaining. It means using positive, respectful words when you are talking to, or about your parents. Your parents are very, very precious to the Lord and He wants you to take care of them and pray for them. He wants you to love them and bless them, as well as those who are guardians, foster parents, or adults who take care of you. People like childcare workers, Sunday school workers, church leaders, aunts, uncles, grandparents, and teachers. Honor all people! Ask God to help you. You can do it!

PRAYER:
Dearest Heavenly Father,
Forgive me for not honoring my parents, or guardians like I should.
Forgive me for dishonoring those who have tried to take care of me.
Help me Lord to do better.
In Jesus' name,
AMEN!

DECLARATION:
(say out loud 3 times)

I HONOR MY MOTHER AND FATHER

> **"May these words of my mouth and this meditation of my heart be pleasing in your sight, Lord, my Rock and my Redeemer."**
> **Psalm 19:14**

IF WE ARE GOING TO BE IN UNITY WITH OTHERS, WE NEED TO WATCH OUR WORDS AND ASK GOD TO EXAMINE OUR HEARTS.

Have you ever heard the saying, "Sticks and stones may break my bones, but names will never hurt me?" Let me ask you something. Do you like it when others call you names? Do you think God likes it? Do you listen to gossip, or have you ever talked about others behind their back? Words hurt. Words have power and if we are saying ugly things about someone, or listening to ugly things about someone, we need to ask why? Before you open your mouth about someone, or spread lies, or rumors about someone, stop and ask yourself if you would like it if someone did that to you? The world needs to see Jesus. The world needs to know Jesus and if the church is fighting and acting like the world, people who are lost in their sins may NEVER, EVER find Him. We must do better. If someone hurts you, go talk to them about it. If you need to, take it to a trusted friend, or adult. If someone hurts you, forgive them and HUSH UNTIL YOU HEAL! Take it to Jesus in prayer and ask Him to help you forgive that person. Ask Him to bless that person and keep loving them, even if you have to love them from a distance. Words are nasty little things.

Make sure the words you use towards yourself and others are life-giving, positive, uplifting words that will build up and not tear down.

PRAYER:
Dear Lord,
Forgive me for gossiping
And saying evil things against others.
Lord, I know that you love everyone
And your don't want me spreading gossip,
Slander, malice or lies about others.
Lord, help me to control my tongue
And help me to forgive others when they hurt me.
In Jesus' name,
AMEN!

DECLARATION:
(say out loud 3 times)

I SPEAK LIFE OVER MYSELF AND OTHERS

TRUST

"Then Peter got down out of the boat, walked on the water and came toward Jesus. But when he saw the wind, he was afraid and, beginning to sink, cried out, "Lord, save me!" Immediately Jesus reached out his hand and caught him. "You of little faith," he said, "Why did you doubt?"
Matthew 14:29-31

TRUST IN GOD

"Do not let your hearts be troubled. You believe in God; believe also in me."
John 14:1

> **"Believe in the Lord Jesus, and you will be saved - you and your household."**
> **Acts 16:31**

TRUSTING GOD MEANS TRUSTING HIS SON, JESUS CHRIST.

In this story in the Bible found in Acts chapter 16, Paul and Silas were two men who loved Jesus with all their hearts and because of their love for Jesus, they told others about Him. For this reason, Paul and Silas were both put in a jail in a place called Rome, but they did not fear, they did not stop trusting in God and they began to sing hymns of praise to God right there in the middle of that horrible jail. There were also other prisoners in their cells listening to Paul and Silas sing about Jesus. It was the middle of the night, midnight to be precise and they sang and sang with love in their hearts to God. Suddenly, an earthquake shook the jail from top to bottom and all the jail cells flung open! Paul and Silas' songs of praise not only helped God to open their cell door, but everyone else's too. A lifestyle of praise and worship affects others, even our own families. We are to be a light of hope to all and sing unto the Lord a song of love and praise. For when we do, the whole world will see, know and believe that Jesus Christ is Lord, just like the jailer who ran to check on the prisoners in this story and threw himself at the feet of Paul and Silas asking in desperation, "What must I do to be saved?" Paul's words still ring true today, as he answered the jailer,

"BELIEVE IN THE LORD JESUS, AND YOU WILL BE SAVED - YOU AND YOUR HOUSEHOLD." Stand for Jesus always. Sing to Him and most importantly, tell others about Him, especially your family.

PRAYER:
Dear Lord,
Thank you for Paul and Silas.
Thank you for saving them and the jailer in this story from Your word, the Bible.
Thank you for showing all of the people in this story, that You alone are God,
You alone are the Holy One, You alone are the Most High, Jesus.
Thank you that even today, this power story is for us and was written for us to know
That you are the King of Glory, You are the All-powerful One and nothing is too
Difficult for you, King Jesus. Nothing.
Help me to believe. Help me to know that when I praise You, I am preparing a place for you to dwell and move and breathe and have Your being through me out towards others.
Fill me with your light. Fill me with your love. King Jesus!
AMEN!

DECLARATION:
(say out loud 3 times)

I TRUST JESUS

> **"Trust in the Lord with all your heart and lean not on your own understanding; in all your ways submit to him, and he will make your paths straight."**
> **Proverbs 3:5,6**

SOMETIMES THINGS SEEM RIGHT, BUT THEY'RE NOT.

In the Bible for instance, God compares wheat and tares in one of his parables, which are stories Jesus told to people to try and help them understand what God's Kingdom is like. You see, wheat and tares are plants that look exactly alike and grow right next to each other, but when the farmer cuts down the wheat for harvest, he separates out the tares from the wheat. The tares, even though they look similar to the wheat, are nothing more than weeds. This is why God tells us here in Proverbs 3:5,6 that we shouldn't lean to our OWN understanding, but to submit to Him, even when we don't understand. God knows where the tares are. He knows that unless we obey His Word, the Bible, we could lose our way, but when we follow Him and keep His Word by obeying His commandments, He will keep us on a straight path. Even when we forget and make mistakes, we can tell God we're sorry and He will forgive us and get us back on the right path, far away from those tricky tares.

PRAYER:
Dearest Lord,
Thank you that You are able to keep me safe from the tares in this world.
You are able to keep me on the right path when I try and do things Your way instead of my own.
Dear Lord, help me to trust you more and more each day.
Help me to remember to read my Bible and do what it says.
In Jesus' name.
AMEN!

DECLARATION:
(say out loud 3 times)

I OBEY THE LORD

> "Commit your way unto the Lord, trust also in Him, and He shall bring it to pass."
> Psalm 37:5

SOMETIMES, THINGS TAKE LONGER THAN WE WOULD LIKE.

For instance, did you ever hear the Bible story about Father Abraham and his wife Sarah? Sarah wasn't able to have children, but one day when she was very old, the angel of the Lord told Abraham that his wife Sarah would become pregnant and have a son and he would be a very special boy because the promises of God would continue through him. His name was Isaac, and God did continue to use Isaac after he was born to share God's promises to the world, but it took Sarah a long time to accept that baby Isaac was coming. In fact, when the angel spoke these things to Abraham about baby Isaac coming, Sarah was in her tent and she laughed. The angel then asked Abraham, "Why did your wife Sarah laugh when I said that she would have a son?" Well, Sarah denied laughing, but she really did laugh. She couldn't understand how she would be able to have a baby when she was almost 90 years old; but just as the angel of the Lord said, Sarah became pregnant one year later and baby Isaac was born when Sarah was 90 years old. Even though at first, Sarah didn't believe it was possible, she eventually committed her way to the Lord and trusted in what the angel said and it surely came to pass. What are you trusting and waiting on God for? Stay committed to His way and He will surely bring it to pass, just like the baby Isaac.

PRAYER:
Dearest Lord and Christ,
Thank you that You help us to walk in Your ways.
Thank you that You know the beginning and the end of everything
So we don't need to be afraid.
Help me Lord to trust You in everything.
I pray this in Your Son, Jesus' name.
AMEN!

DECLARATION:
(say out loud 3 times)

I COMMIT MY WAY UNTO THE LORD

> "Therefore I tell you, do not worry about your life, what you will eat or drink; or about your body, what you will wear. Is not life more than food, and the body more than clothes? Look at the birds of the air; they do not sow or reap or store away in barns, and yet your heavenly Father feeds them."
> Matthew 6:25-26

HAVE YOU EVER HEARD THE SAYING, "THINGS HAVE A WAY OF WORKING THEMSELVES OUT?"

Well, it's true. God has a way of bringing good out of everything, even the bad stuff and He wants us to trust Him and stop worrying. Worrying doesn't help, it only makes us nervous and anxious. God doesn't want that for us. He wants us to pray, He wants us to thank HIm, He wants us to sing Him a song and just give all of our troubles and cares to Him because He is big enough to carry all our problems. The next time you start to worry, say a prayer instead. The next time you're tempted to worry, sing a song to Jesus instead. Maybe pretend that you are giving all your cares to Jesus in a big box and handing it to Him and in your mind's eye, you see Jesus carrying away all your troubles because He cares for you. So, worry less and pray more. God is so mighty and He's a big, big God. He can handle all your troubles, cares and needs. He loves you. Talk to Him about it.

PRAYER:
Dear Lord,
Forgive me when I worry and don't trust you like I should.
Forgive me when I complain, or want what others have.
Lord, help me to ask you for the things I need and want.
I know I can trust you with my life.
In Jesus' name.
AMEN!

DECLARATION:
(say out loud 3 times)

I WILL PRAY AND NOT WORRY

> **"Jesus Christ is the same yesterday and today and forever."**
> **Hebrews 13:8**

THIS SCRIPTURE IS ONE OF MY FAVORITES!

Do you want to know why? I'll tell you why. I love this scripture because it tells us so much about what Jesus is like. He NEVER, EVER changes. His message of love and forgiveness never, ever changes. He died to set us free from the penalty of sin and when we trust in what He did for us on the cross, we can be set free and live with Him FOREVER in ETERNITY! What a Savior! This free gift is yours for the asking. As long as you live on planet Earth, you can call on the name of Jesus and have your sins washed away and start over. You can call on His name every time you make a mistake and tell Him you're sorry and He will always, always forgive you. He never, ever changes and His love for you never, ever changes either. Do you know Jesus for yourself? Have you asked Him to forgive you for all your sins and save you from what's to come. You don't need to be afraid if you have put your trust in Jesus and because He never changes, He will see you safely to Heaven and help you while you live here on Earth. Call upon His name, go to church, read your Bible, especially when hard things happen. He will help you. He loves you and His love for you never, ever changes no matter what you do wrong.

PRAYER:
Dear Lord,
Thank you that you are the same
Yesterday, today and FOREVER!
Thank you that I can trust You to save me and keep me close.
Thank you that no matter what, You always love me.
Lord, please help me to stay close to You.
Help me to call upon your name every time I make a mistake.
Lord, please help me to come to You and never hide from You,
But to come to You for all my needs, hopes and plans.
In Jesus' name.
AMEN!

DECLARATION:
(say out loud 3 times)

JESUS NEVER CHANGES

> **"And my God will meet all your needs according to the riches of his glory in Christ Jesus."**
> **Philippians 4:19**

WE ALL HAVE NEEDS.

Every human being all over the world has the same needs. Things like love, shelter (a place to live), clothes, shoes, schooling, food and water. People everywhere need these things to live. These things aren't the same as our WANTS. A want is different than a need. A want is something we can live without like a new bike, or a new video game. A need is something that we cannot live without. Think about it. Food and water are things that you cannot live without or you will die. Medicine can be like this, too. Maybe you have asthma and need an inhaler, or maybe you're a diabetic and you need your insulin. Without these life-giving medicines, you could die. Well, there is another way humans can die, too. They can be eternally separated from God when they don't put their trust in Jesus Christ. They could be the richest person in the world, but not get to Heaven because they refused God's free gift of trusting in Jesus. Every human being NEEDS TO BE SAVED! You see, without trusting in Jesus, you can never be healed of spiritual death. Someday, your spirit will leave this world and it NEEDS JESUS to get it to Heaven. This NEED is met when you trust in Jesus and what He did on the cross for you. Believe in Him and be saved. He will meet your physical needs while here on the Earth and He has already met your spiritual need for redemption in the next life, too. He has made a way for you to have the true riches. The riches of His eternal home in Heaven. Follow Jesus all your life. He is working through His church to reach the whole world with the message of Heaven.

PRAYER:
Dear Lord Jesus,
Help me to trust You with my life.
Help me to know You more and more.
Help me to not only trust You,
But to also tell others about You.
Help me to be brave like You.
Help me to not worry, but to trust and obey
Your voice all my life.
I ask these things through Jesus Christ,
My Lord.
AMEN!

DECLARATION:
(say out loud 3 times)

JESUS IS THE WAY TO HEAVEN

> "And we know that in all things God works for the good of those who love him, who have been called according to his purpose."
> **Romans 8:28**

BUTTERFLIES HAVE A GREAT LESSON TO TEACH US!

Before a butterfly is a butterfly, it is a caterpillar. While it is still a caterpillar, the caterpillar puts a house around its body called a cocoon. The cocoon protects the caterpillar from harm while it lives in the cocoon and slowly changes into a butterfly. The caterpillar chooses carefully where to place its cocoon so that it can turn into a butterfly with no interruptions. Places like trees, leaves and bushes are usually where the caterpillar goes to build its cocoon but, here is a very important fact. If you interrupt the cocoon one minute before its time, the caterpillar will die and never become a beautiful butterfly. The caterpillar must complete the full two weeks in the cocoon and then STRUGGLE to break open the cocoon ON ITS OWN. If you try to help the butterfly as it is trying to break out of the cocoon, it will die. The struggle to break out of its cocoon is part of the process in making the caterpillar beautiful and ready to fly when it emerges from the cocoon. God uses the struggle in the caterpillar's cocoon, to bring forth an amazing and wonderful change. Instead of just inching along, now the caterpillar has developed beautiful wings to fly with and all because God uses

ALL things in the butterfly's life to bring about a good outcome. This is what He does for us, too. The hard stuff is what helps us learn to fly so don't ever give up. God will use even the bad stuff to bring good into your life and He will use those hard places to make you into the butterfly that you are supposed to be.

PRAYER:
Dearest Lord Jesus,
Thank you that all things work together for Good
Of those who love You and have been called
According to Your purpose.
Lord, I know that I can trust you to
Bring about the changes in my life
That will help me be stronger and
Will help me become the person You
Want me to be.
Thank you Lord for helping
Me to be my best me.
In Jesus' name I pray.
AMEN!

DECLARATION:
(say out loud 3 times)

ALL THINGS WORK TOGETHER FOR GOOD

> **"Have I not commanded you? Be strong and courageous. Do not be afraid; do not be discouraged, for the Lord your God will be with you wherever you go."**
> **Joshua 1:7**

RIGHT BEFORE JESUS KNEW HE WAS ABOUT TO DIE FOR OUR SINS, HE WAS FEELING VERY DISHEARTENED AND SAD.

Some people think that Jesus was afraid when He knew that the soldiers were coming to get Him, but that's not exactly what the Bible says. The Bible says that Jesus was filled with sorrow, or sadness when He knew His time to die had come. You see, Jesus loves people so much. He even loved the soldiers who came and took Him away to die on the cross for our sins. Jesus felt sad, not afraid when the soldiers came to get Him because His heart ached with love for those soldiers. He longed for them to love Him too, but instead they took him away to die a painful death on a Roman cross and while He hung there in agony, He cried out, "Father, forgive them, for they do not know what they are doing." Perfect love casts out fear. Love is always more powerful than fear and Jesus' love can make you strong, too. Be brave. Trust Jesus. He will see you through your hard times.

PRAYER:
Dear Jesus,
Thank you for dying on the cross for my sins.
Thank you for doing what you did so that I can live with you
Here on Earth and one day in Heaven.
Help me pray for others.
Help me love others like you do.
Help me to be brave and strong
So that I can tell others about Your Great Love!
I ask it all in Your Name.
AMEN!

DECLARATION:
(say out loud 3 times)

JESUS DIED FOR ME

> "You will keep in perfect peace those whose minds are steadfast, because they trust in you."
> Isaiah 26:3

DO YOU KNOW WHO Corrie ten Boom WAS?

She was a woman who lived in the country of Holland during World War II when the German army invaded Holland and took over. Maybe you have learned about World War II in school. It was a terrible time when a man named Adolf Hitler was trying to ultimately conquer the world and He was hurting a lot of people, especially Jewish people. Hitler was gathering up the Jewish people in Holland, too and taking them to places called concentration camps where they had to work very hard with very little food or water. Many Jewish people died or were put to death and by the end of World War II, over Six million Jewish people had been slaughtered by Adolf Hitler's army known as the Nazi's. Corrie and her family loved the Jewish people and tried to help save them, but the Nazi's found out and Corrie and her family were sent away to the prison camps just like the Jewish people. Eventually, Corrie and her sister Betsie were taken to the prison camp of Ravensbruck in Germany where the guards would make the entire prison camp get up at 3:30am and stand in the freezing cold until 6:30am. For those three hours every morning the female prisoners would have to stand completely still while the guards would hurt the prisoners in unspeakable ways. Corrie ten Boom said that the only way she and her sister, Betsie and some of the other prisoners made it through those difficult times were that they would watch a beautiful bird called a Lark that would come each morning to sing to them. Corrie said that as long as she kept her eyes and thoughts on that bird, she was able to find peace in the storm she was facing. Jesus is like that Lark. Looking to and trusting in Jesus brings perfect peace into our lives no matter what we are facing.

PRAYER:
Dear Lord,
Thank you that you keep me
In perfect peace when I keep my thoughts on You.
Help me to do that no matter what I am facing.
In Jesus' name.
AMEN!

DECLARATION:
(say out loud 3 times)

JESUS IS MY PEACE

> **"Blessed is the one who trusts in the Lord, who does not look to the proud, to those who turn aside to false gods."**
> **Psalms 40:4**

WHAT THINGS DO YOU PUT YOUR TRUST IN?

Maybe you trust your friend, or your mom or dad. Maybe you trust in looking good by wearing the best clothes or the best shoes. Maybe you trust in how many followers you have on your favorite social network page. Maybe you put your faith in how much money you have, or what kind of car you or your parents drive. Maybe you think that going on a lot of vacations is the way to happiness. Psalm 40:4 tells us here and elsewhere in the Bible that the best person to trust for everything and in every situation in the Lord Jesus. He is the one who will never leave us or forsake us and He is the one who holds tomorrow in His hands. Go to Him first for everything. Don't put your faith in things that can get broken or lost or stolen. Put your faith and trust in the One True and Living God who knows everything, sees everything and can take good care of you if you will only trust Him.

PRAYER:
Dear Lord,
Please forgive me when I have looked to
People and things for my trust instead of You.
Help me, Lord to not pride myself in things,
But to put my faith and trust in You only.
Help me to have no other gods before You!
In Jesus' name.
AMEN!

DECLARATION:
(say out loud 3 times)

I TURN TO GOD FIRST

> "When I am afraid, I put my trust in you. In God, whose word I praise - in God I trust and am not afraid. What can mere mortals do to me?"
> Psalms 56:3-4

EVERYONE GETS AFRAID SOMETIMES.

It's true. Sometimes we feel afraid, but when we refocus on God He can give us courage and help us to trust Him. Just like we refocus the lens on a camera, or a pair of binoculars to help us see better, we can refocus our attention on Jesus to help us take our focus off the fear and onto Jesus. This is what I do whenever I fly in an airplane. I don't really like to fly and there used to be a day when I would really get afraid, but then I learned to remember the scripture above whenever I got on an airplane. I learned to sing a song of worship, or pray, or anything to help me focus on Jesus when I am flying on an airplane. These spiritual exercises have helped me to feel peaceful during times of fear and have helped me to remember to trust Jesus in everything. Remember, fear can be redirected to faith. It's all in how you look at it. What are you focused on? Focus on Jesus. You can trust Him and remember this acronym:

F.E.A.R. = **F**alse **E**vidence **A**ppearing **R**eal

PRAYER:
Dear Lord,
Thank you that I can trust You.
Thank you that You are bigger and stronger and
When I focus on You, I can overcome my fears and doubts.
Lord, help me to look to You and do it afraid if I have to,
But Lord, help me to do what you need me to.
I trust that as I step out in faith, you will help me
Get stronger and stronger.
In Jesus' name I pray.
AMEN!

DECLARATION:
(say out loud 3 times)

WHEN I AM AFRAID I WILL TRUST YOU

> "For I know the plans I have for you, declares the Lord, plans to prosper you and not to harm you, plans to give you hope and a future."
> Jeremiah 29:11

JEREMIAH WAS JUST A TEENAGER WHEN GOD CALLED HIM TO BE A PROPHET TO THE NATIONS.

Jeremiah was very reluctant to follow the Lord in what the Lord had called him to do because He thought that He was too young and He was afraid to go and speak the truth to people because He knew they would get mad at him. But God kept working with Jeremiah and reminding Jeremiah that even before Jeremiah was born, God knew him, God saw Jeremiah in His mind's eye. He could see that beautiful baby, Jeremiah even before he was born and God started making plans for him. He gave him just the right parents, made him be born at just the right time and in just the right town so that Jeremiah could do all the plans God had for him. You, my friend, are like this too. God loves you as much as He loved Jeremiah and He has a very specific plan for your life. Maybe you'll be a scientist, a doctor, a nurse, or teacher. Maybe you'll be a mechanic, or engineer, or parent. Maybe you'll be a pastor, or missionary who travels all over the world. Maybe you'll write children's books, or books about the Bible to help people grow in their faith. Whatever you were born to do, you can trust that God's plan is best for you. You can trust Him to give you hope in all the hard times and you can trust Him to bring you into your future with Him by your side. Keep trusting God your whole life through. He knows the plans He has for you. Just partner with Him in prayer and ask Him what to do each day. He will show you.

PRAYER:
Dearest Lord,
I know that You have specific plans for me.
I know that you want to prosper me,
To help me and bring me hope when I need it.
I know that you have a good future for me.
Please help me Lord, to do what is right.
Help me to seek you in prayer for all of my decisions.
In Jesus' name.
AMEN!

DECLARATION:
(say out loud 3 times)

GOD'S PLAN FOR ME IS BEST

> **"There is no fear in love. But perfect love drives out fear, because fear has to do with punishment. The one who fears is not made perfect in love."**
> **1 John 4:18**

GOD IS LOVE AND THE MORE YOU GET TO KNOW HIM, THE MORE YOU WILL SEE THAT HIS LOVE IS PERFECT.

God loves us so much. He loves us with something known as "AGAPE" love. Agape love is unconditional love. This means that God loves us no matter what and nothing can separate us from His love. Not height, nor depth; length, or width. Not things gone by, or things to come, not even life or death can separate us from His love. He loves us all the same and His love is not based on what you do or don't do. His love is so pure that there is no fear in it. His love is so powerful and so amazing that it casts all the fear out, all the darkness out. His love is what drove Him to the cross because He stopped at nothing to save us. He loved us so much He knew what He had to do. Only His perfect love for us could wash us and make us new.

PRAYER:
Dear God in Heaven,
Thank you for Your perfect Love.
Thank you that Your love casts out all fear
And makes me whole and new when I trust in You.
Lord, help me to love you more by loving others more.
Help me to tell others about Your great Love
On the cross of Calvary.
Thank you for dying for my sins
And the sins of the whole world.
Your love is everlasting.
It goes on and on.
In Jesus' name.
AMEN!

DECLARATION:
(say out loud 3 times)

GOD'S LOVE NEVER ENDS

TRUSTING OTHERS

"No temptation has overtaken you except what is common to mankind. And God is faithful; he will not let you be tempted beyond what you can bear. But when you are tempted, he will also provide a way out so that you can endure it."
1 Corinthians 10:13

NOTES

> **"For all have sinned and fall short of the glory of God."**
> **Romans 3:23**

AS WE LOOK AT TRUSTING OTHERS, WE MUST REMEMBER ROMANS 3:23.

The Bible is clear that all of us miss the mark. We are not perfect and we shouldn't expect others to be perfect either, but we can learn to be a person people can count on. After you've given your heart and life to Jesus Christ, you must learn how to be a trustworthy person. You must learn to keep your word to the best of your ability. When you tell someone you will do something, don't go back on it. Follow through, even if other people don't. Be the person that shows up and does what they say they will do. When you tell your friend that you will hang out with them, or help them with their homework, do it. Don't change your mind just because your feelings change. I remember a time when I told my friend that I would take her sightseeing in New York City. My friend had never visited New York City before and she was nervous about the busy streets and tall buildings. She really needed someone to help her get around the city safely and I told my friend that I would help her, but there was a problem. I had to stop doing something I enjoyed and travel all the way back to my apartment to meet up with my friend so that I could help her. It was hard and part of me wanted to cancel on my friend at the last minute, but I thought of her standing in front of my apartment waiting for me to show up. We didn't have cell phones then. She would have been all by herself and probably very frightened. I couldn't do that to my friend. So, I stopped what I was doing and kept my word to my friend. It was hard, but looking back, I'm really glad that I took good care of my friend, instead of thinking only of myself.

PRAYER:
Dear Heavenly Father,
Thank you for your Son, Jesus
Thank you that because of Him, we can all be forgiven
Help me Lord to remember Romans 3:23
Help me to be kind and gentle with others
Help me to be a trustworthy person like your Son, Jesus
I pray these things in Your name, Lord
AMEN!

DECLARATION:
(say out loud 3 times)

WITH GOD'S HELP, I AM A TRUSTWORTHY PERSON

> **"For the flesh desires what is contrary to the Spirit, and the Spirit what is contrary to the flesh. They are in conflict with each other, so that you are not to do whatever you want."**
> **Galatians 5:17**

HAVE YOU EVER PLAYED TUG-OF WAR?

In case you haven't, Tug-of-war is a game that is played usually with two teams and a very large, long rope. A brightly colored scarf or bandana is tied exactly in the middle of the long rope and both teams line up to grab a hold of each side of the rope with the scarf dividing the two teams. There are usually the same amount of rope holders on each side of the scarf and when the signal is given, both teams begin to pull. The first team to pull the opposite team over to their side is the winner. Tug-of-war is a great way to not only have some fun, but to also help demonstrate the battle that we all have sometimes in our lives. All human beings are three parts. They are body, soul and spirit. Our body (or "flesh") is often at times in a war with the spirit. The spirit side of things are things like love, joy, peace, patience, kindness, goodness, gentleness, faithfulness and self-control. The fleshly side of us can be things like wanting our own way, having a temper tantrum, being unkind, lying, cheating, stealing. Sometimes we know the right thing to do, but our flesh takes over and we let our own desires win out. That is why we see that in the scripture above it says that the flesh and the spirit are contrary to one another. This means that just like in a Tug-of-war game, two sides are pulling back and forth. When it comes to everyday life, it's up to you which side wins. You must choose which side you'll give in to. The good news is, when you feel like you're going to make a wrong choice, you can pray and ask God to help you.

PRAYER:
Dearest Lord and Savior,
I'm sorry for the times when I have given into what I want
Instead of following Your Spirit.
Help me to follow Your Spirit more and more
And to learn to say no to evil temptations
Through Jesus Christ our Lord, I pray
AMEN!

DECLARATION:
(say out loud 3 times)

I WILL BE LED BY THE SPIRIT

> "The heart is deceitful above all things and beyond cure. Who can understand it? I the Lord search the heart and examine the mind, to reward each person according to their conduct, according to what their deeds deserve."
> Jeremiah 17:9-10

WHEN MY CHILDREN WERE SMALL, I SANG A SONG TO THEM.

The words of the song went something like this: Oh be careful little eyes what you see. Oh be careful little ears what you hear. Oh be careful little mouth what you say. Oh be careful little heart whom you trust. Oh be careful little mind what you think. Oh be careful little hands what you do. Oh be careful little feet where you go. For the Father up above is looking down in love so, be careful little one what you do. What we feed our hearts will come out in our speech and actions. When you look at evil, it affects your heart. When you watch scary TV shows, it affects your heart and mind. When you go places you shouldn't, it affects your heart. When you read things that go against the Bible, it affects your heart. Everything you do, say and think, affects your heart. This is why God tells us to feed our hearts with His Word, the Bible. He tells us to go to church on a regular basis to help tune our hearts to His Spirit. He tells us how to keep our hearts right by keeping our focus on Him throughout the day. We can do this by singing a song to Him, by praying, reading our Bible or doing something kind for someone. Because our hearts are spiritually sick due to our sin nature (we naturally want the opposite of what God says is good), we need Jesus to cleanse our hearts daily. When we tell Jesus each day that we are sorry for our sins, He cleanses our hearts and makes us whole again, but we must talk with Him daily about our sins. Going to Jesus like this, is like taking a spiritual bath. You can take a spiritual shower every day and get your insides all nice and clean again. If you want to, Jesus can help you live His way.

PRAYER:
Dearest Lord,
I know that my heart is spiritually sick without You.
Please forgive me for any sin in my life and help me to turn from it.
Help me Lord to turn from all sin and live Your Way.
In Jesus' name,
AMEN!

DECLARATION:
(say out loud 3 times)

MY HEART IS FOR JESUS

> "Now while he was in Jerusalem at the Passover Festival, many people saw the signs he was performing and believed in his name. But Jesus would not entrust himself to them, for he knew all people. He did not need any testimony about mankind, for he knew what was in each person."
> John 2:23-24

I REMEMBER SOMETHING THAT HAPPENED TO SOMEONE CLOSE TO ME.

I know of a young lady whose mother was an alcoholic. This mother would drink heavily every day, causing her daughter a lot of anxiety and pain, as well as the rest of her family.

It wasn't until the mother almost died in a car accident that the mother's life changed. I remember before the accident, listening to the daughter say how she couldn't trust her mother. She shared over and over how her mother had disappointed her and not kept her promise to stop her drinking. While this daughter lost trust in her mother, she could still pray for her and love her. This is what Jesus did. He knew that people's hearts were full of sin and liable to sin at any time. Jesus knew that even a person who knew Him, could struggle in their heart and be prone to sin. This is why He came. To shed light on the darkness hidden in the heart of every person.

PRAYER:
Dear Lord,
You did not trust the hearts of people.
You knew that people's hearts are full of sin
And even those who follow You need a lot of help in their hearts.
Lord, please help me to know You more.
Help me to know Your Word, the Bible, more
So that I might not sin against You.
In Your name I pray,
AMEN!

DECLARATION:
(say out loud 3 times)

MY HEART TRUSTS YOU LORD

> **"Create in me a pure heart, O God, and renew a steadfast spirit within me."**
> **Psalm 51:10**

AS WE LOOK AT TRUSTING OTHERS IN THIS SECTION OF OUR DEVOTIONAL, WE SEE SEVERAL THINGS.

Jeremiah 17:9 tells us that the human heart is deceitful above all things and beyond cure. John 2:24 tells us that not even JESUS trusted His heart to people. Jesus knew the human heart could not be trusted and that is why He gave us Psalm 51:10. He wants us to come to Him and pray and ask Him to change our hearts. He wants us to do this daily. He wants us to ask for His help always and in everything to keep the right motives for doing things. If you do things for any other reason than to love and worship God, chances are your heart is getting the best of you again and you need to go to the Lord for help. Why you do something, is as important as what you do. Whatever you do, ask the Lord to help you to do it with the right heart and spirit. For Him. Only for Him. People will let you down. They may not want to. They may not mean to. But they will! And you will let down. This is all part of being human. The thing to remember is that Jesus will never let you down. You can trust Him. Serve Him today and everyday! He is so worthy of all we can give.

PRAYER:
Dear Lord Jesus,
My heart needs you.
Because I am human, I make mistakes.
Sometimes I want to hurt others on purpose, too.
I'm sorry Lord. Please forgive me
And give me a heart like yours.
Create in me everyday a heart that is clean,
A heart that is pure, a heart that loves and serves You.
Keep my spirit steady for You Lord.
Help me to go to church, read my Bible
And to pray.
I love you, Lord.
In Jesus' name,
AMEN!

DECLARATION:
(say out loud 3 times)

MY HEART IS PURE FOR JESUS

> **"Whatever you do, work at it with all your heart, as working for the Lord, not for human masters, since you know that you will receive an inheritance from the Lord as a reward."**
> **Colossians 3:23,24**

WHATEVER YOU DO, DO IT FOR JESUS!

I recently visited the Billy Graham Library in Charlotte, North Carolina. If you don't know who Billy Graham was, you need to. Billy Graham was a man that lived to nearly 100 years old and who spent most of his life telling others about Jesus Christ and how He died for their sins, encouraging one and all to trust Jesus and live forever. Millions of people came to know Jesus Christ because of the life of Billy Graham. Everything he did, he did for Jesus. Whether it was preaching, teaching, traveling, raising his children, or just taking a walk, Billy Graham did it all for Christ. His wife, Ruth did this too. We watched a news clip of her telling the audience that everything she did, she did as "unto the Lord." Making a bed, cleaning the house, cooking dinner, reading her Bible, or praying for her very busy husband. It was all done with Jesus in mind. This is truly the best way to live. People won't appreciate what you do, but Jesus sure will. He is such a wonderful Savior. So, whatever you do, do it for Jesus. Do it as, "unto the Lord." Whether it is doing your homework, playing baseball, or just resting at home. Do it with Jesus in mind. This will keep your heart happy and free from complaining.

PRAYER:
Dearest Jesus,
I'm so sorry when I complain, or try to do things to impress others.
I know now that your Word, the Bible tells me
That I am to do everything as, "unto YOU!"
Please help me to live this way.
Please help me to live for YOU.
I ask this in Your name,
AMEN!

DECLARATION:
(say out loud 3 times)

I DO IT ALL FOR JESUS

> **"Anyone who does wrong will be repaid for their wrongs, and there is no favoritism."**
> **Colossians 3:25**

IN GOD'S KINGDOM THERE ARE NO FAVORITES.

God is the only one that is so big and powerful that He can love everyone in the whole world the same. He doesn't love the people who behave well more than He loves the people who misbehave. He loves everyone the same. This doesn't mean that He likes the sinful things people do. God HATES sin because it is sin that separates us from Him, but as long as we have put our trust in Jesus Christ as our Savior, we can ask God for forgiveness as often as we need to and he will ALWAYS forgive us. He is such an amazing God who loves us all and you don't have to worry about people getting away with anything. God sees when people commit a sin, but He tries to help people realize the error of their ways. Sometimes He brings consequences to help them turn from sin. Sometimes He allows circumstances, or sometimes He tries to speak to them in a small, still voice to warn them. This small, still voce is what the world calls your, "conscience." Whatever the case may be, God loves us all the same and He will correct those who treat us badly. We can trust Him to do this, even when we can't trust others.

PRAYER:
Dear Lord,
Thank you that You love us all the same.
Thank you that You don't love one person more than another.
Thank you that when we sin, or when others sin,
We can trust that you will take care of it in Your time
And in Your way.
Help me to trust you in this, Lord.
In Your name I pray,
AMEN!

DECLARATION:
(say out loud 3 times)

GOD LOVES ME

> **"You will keep in perfect peace those whose minds are steadfast, because they trust in you."**
> **Isaiah 26:3**

HAVE YOU EVER BEEN AFRAID?

Have you ever had someone hurt you, or betray you and not want to be your friend anymore? Have you had to face something that was hard for you? The Bible tells us in Isaiah 26:3 that if we will think about the Lord and keep our mind and thoughts on Him, He will give us the peace we need. Trusting the Lord no matter what, is the key to everything you do in life because we have already established in some of the other devotional writings that people cannot really be trusted fully. People can learn to control their selfish tendencies and learn to be more trustworthy, but ultimately, we will all let each other down. This is where God's grace and mercy come in. We learn to forgive others for the Lord's sake and for the sake of keeping peace in our hearts and minds. When we learn to think about Jesus in every situation of life, we will have peace and we will know what to do, creating a steady way of walking close to Him all of our lives. It takes time, maturity and practice so don't give up. You can do it! If you make a mistake, tell the Lord you're sorry and keep going.

PRAYER:
Dear Lord,
Please help me to keep my thoughts on You,
Especially when I am afraid, or when I
Am having a hard day.
Please turn my heart and mind to You
Whenever I need You to.
I ask this in Jesus' name,
AMEN!

DECLARATION:
(say out loud 3 times)

I THINK ABOUT THE LORD

> "Finally, brothers and sisters, whatever is true, whatever is noble, whatever is right, whatever is pure, whatever is lovely, whatever is admirable - if anything is excellent or praiseworthy - think about such things."
> **Philippians 4:8**

HAVE YOU EVER HEARD THE OLD SAYING, "YOU ARE WHAT YOU EAT?"

This means that whatever food you eat each day will affect you. Too much junk and candy can give you a stomachache and as you get older could really affect your physical health. Your mind works the same way. In essence, "YOU ARE WHAT YOU THINK ABOUT." If you focus on negative thoughts about yourself and others, then you will make yourself and others feel bad. Thoughts are like food for the brain. You are either feeding your brain good food thoughts, or bad food thoughts. Stay away from negativity. Feed your brain beautiful, true, noble, right, pure, lovely, admirable, excellent and praiseworthy thoughts all day long. Read your Bible daily and feed your mind with the Word of God. Reshape, recharge and refocus your thought life. You'll be happy you did! As a person thinks, so shall they be!

PRAYER:
Dear Lord,
Thank you that I have the power
To choose my thoughts.
I can choose to think about good things
That will help me be strong in my mind.
I can also ask You, Lord
To take the negative thoughts away.
I ask you today, to help me
To keep my heart,
Mind and thoughts
Fixed on You, Lord.
I ask it in Your name.
AMEN!

DECLARATION:
(say out loud 3 times)

I THINK GOD THOUGHTS

> **"There is a way that appears to be right, but in the end it leads to death."**
> **Proverbs 14:12**

HAVE YOU EVER WANTED TO DO SOMETHING BECAUSE EVERYONE ELSE WAS?

I remember when I was a young person, a really scary movie about sharks came out in the movie theaters and everyone was going to see it. When I asked my mother if I could go see this movie, she told me that she felt it would be too scary for me. She told me that because we spent our summer vacations at the beach, she felt it might negatively affect my summer activities with my family. But all my friends were going to see the movie and the ratings said that I was old enough to see it. The thing is, my mother knew ME. She knew that this sort of movie would be way too much for me. In the end, she was right and I am scared of sharks to this very day. Never again was I able to enjoy swimming in the ocean. Proverbs 14:12 is so true. There is a way that may seem right and may even BE right for someone else, but that doesn't mean that it is right for you. Trust the people closest to you. They know you best. Never make a decision based on other people's opinions or choices. Make your own choices. Choose what is best for you. Ask the Lord to help you make the right choices in your life. You'll save yourself a lot of anguish if you do.

PRAYER:
Dearest Lord,
Please help me to know what is best for me.
Help me to make the right choices in my life.
Help me to follow You, not people.
Help me to learn to say no when needed.
Help me to see that it is okay to do something
Different from what my friends are doing.
I ask in Your name Lord,
Jesus.
AMEN!

DECLARATION:
(say out loud 3 times)

I CHOOSE WHAT IS BEST FOR ME

> "One who has unreliable friends soon comes to ruin, but there is a friend who sticks closer than a brother."
> Proverbs 18:24

MANY YEARS AGO, I HAD A FRIEND WHOM I LOVED MORE THAN ANYTHING.

We had so much fun together and had many sleepovers and adventures together until one day, my friend started hanging out with another girl. They were both taking the same gymnastics class together and spending a lot of time together. I tried joining gymnastics too, so that I could still be close to my friend, however, I didn't really like gymnastics and she was very into this new girl. For a while, all three of us hung out, but I got tired of being the third wheel, so I was forced to make new friends which is very hard when you're in middle school. Since that time, I have had many friends. Some good, others not so good, but through it all I have learned a valuable lesson. Just like it says in Proverbs 18:24, Jesus is the friend that sticks closer than a brother and He never leaves us nor forsakes us. Never permit others to undervalue you. You are precious to the Lord. More precious than diamonds and rubies. He wants you with people who don't mistreat you, but if they do, Jesus will be there every time.

PRAYER:
Dear Lord,
Thank you that You are my friend.
Thank you that You stick closer than a brother.
Thank you that You value me
And love me.
Please send good people into
My life to be my friend.
In Jesus' name,
AMEN!

DECLARATION:
(say out loud 3 times)

JESUS IS MY FRIEND AND BROTHER

> "I know what it is to be in need, and I know what it is to have plenty. I have learned the secret of being content in any and every situation, whether well fed or hungry, whether living in plenty or in want. I can do all this through him who gives me strength."
> Philippians 4:12-3

NO MATTER WHAT, YOU CAN DO ALL THINGS THROUGH CHRIST!

When my kids were young, I taught them Philippians 4:13. I had them memorize it like this: "I can do ALL things through Christ who strengthens me." Whenever they complained, or whined and said they couldn't do something, I'd have them recite Philippians 4:13. Whenever they were facing something that seemed too hard for them, I had them recite Philippians 4:13. To this day, I will sometimes remind them to say this scripture over their lives and circumstances when I see them struggling with something. I encourage you to do the same and memorize Philippians 4:13 for yourself. Notice that God tells us here that we can do ALL things through Him who gives us strength. This means ALL things, not just SOME things. I challenge you to use this scripture every chance you get. The Word of God, the Bible is a tool. It is called the SWORD of the Spirit. Use it to fight off doubt. Use it over and over until you feel faith rise up in you. Faith to move mountains is possible when we activate our faith using God's Word.

PRAYER:
Dearest Lord and Savior,
Please forgive me when I have not been
Content with what I have.
Please help me to use Your Word
To overcome whatever comes my way.
In Jesus' name,
AMEN!

DECLARATION:
(say out loud 3 times)

I CAN DO ALL THINGS THROUGH CHRIST WHO STRENGTHENS ME

> **"My grace is sufficient for you, for my power is made perfect in weakness. Therefore I will boast all the more gladly about my weaknesses, so that Christ's power may rest on me."**
> **2 Corinthians 12:9**

GOD'S WAYS ARE MUCH DIFFERENT THAN OURS!

Sometimes it seems like God's Kingdom is an upside-down Kingdom. In God's economy of doing things, He is most strong in us when we are at our weakest moments. This is because, when we are feeling weak, we see our need for God. Sometimes, the only time people reach out for God is when they feel weak, sad, hurt, or sick. It is at these times, when God is able to show us just how much He cares and how He is always with us. I remember when I first gave my heart to Jesus, it was after I had gone through a difficult time. Instead of getting angry about my difficulty, I started to look to God for help. Prior to this time, I think I believed God was real, but I didn't know Him for myself. It was through my weakness, that God was able to show Himself to me. He helped me in my difficulty, and I was able to see how strong God really is. If the difficulty never happened, how would I have known God's strength for myself. This was what made me want to be a Christian and live for Jesus. I'm so grateful that in my weakness, He was made strong.

PRAYER:
Dear Lord,
Thank you for Your grace.
Thank you for Your might and power.
Thank you for saving me.
Thank you for loving me.
Help me to be trust You and be happy
When things are difficult
Because I know that when I am weak
You are made strong.
In Your name I pray, Lord,
Jesus.
AMEN!

DECLARATION:
(say out loud 3 times)

WHEN I AM WEAK HE IS STRONG

CAMARADERIE:

Merriam-Webster.com defines camaraderie as: a feeling of friendship, goodwill and familiarity among the people in a group. It also goes on to say that the word camaraderie is taken from the French word camarade, meaning COMRADE.

Some other words with similar meanings:

Brotherhood
Sisterhood
Community
Company
Fellowship
Chumminess
Companionship
Togetherness
Society
Companion

CAMARADERIE WITH GOD
"Behold, I stand at the door and knock; if anyone hears My voice and opens the door, I will come in to him and will dine with him, and he with Me."
Revelation 3:20

> **"And the scripture was fulfilled that says, 'Abraham believed God, and it was credited to him as righteousness,' and he was called God's friend."**
> **James 2:23**

ABRAHAM WAS THE PERSON THAT GOD CHOSE TO ESTABLISH AN IMPORTANT CONTRACT WITH.

When you trust God like Abraham did, you can be God's friend, too. God made a pact (known as a covenant, or contract) with Abraham that said that through Abraham, God would bless the WHOLE WORLD and that Abraham's descendants would be as numerous as the stars in the sky. Have you ever heard that old church song called, "Father Abraham?" Well, the reason we call him FATHER ABRAHAM is because it was through Abraham that God was able to bring us the Good News about Jesus dying on the cross to forgive us of our sins. All the people born from Abraham to Jesus showed us the way to salvation in Jesus Christ. That's amazing! Yes, God chose Abraham because Abraham trusted God to the point of being willing to sacrifice his only son, Isaac. God knew that Abraham was devoted to him because of his willingness to give God the one thing he loved the most, his son, Isaac. Abraham was a man of great faith. He left his country and moved to a new one when God asked him to. He waited a long time to have his son, Isaac because God asked him to and he was willing to give Isaac up, if God said to. In the end, God relented and didn't require Abraham to give Isaac up. Abraham's willingness to give Isaac up was enough for God to know that Abraham was His friend. Are you God's friend? Are you willing to follow His instructions in the Bible? Do you love God like Abraham did? God called Abraham His friend. I hope He can say the same of you.

PRAYER:
Dear Lord,
Thank you for Father Abraham.
Thank you for his example.
Help me to be like him.
I want to have faith like him.
I ask to have obedience like him.
Make me more like Abraham, Lord.
In Jesus' name,
AMEN!

DECLARATION:
(say out loud 3 times)

I OBEY AND HAVE GREAT FAITH IN GOD

"But Noah found favor in the eyes of the Lord."
Genesis 6:8

WE KNOW THAT NOAH BUILT THE ARK.

Fellowship with God means doing the thing that others may say is impossible. The ark was a very large boat that God had Noah and his family build to keep them alive during the Great Flood. Most people laughed at Noah and his family, saying it couldn't be done. They thought that Noah was crazy to build a giant boat because, "God told him to," but we know that the rain came and the earth flooded just like Noah said it would. Two of every animal, both male and female were kept alive on the ark as well as Noah and his family (his wife, three sons and their wives). The entire process took about one year before they could come out of the ark onto DRY ground. That's when God put a rainbow in the sky as a sign to Noah and his family that He would never again flood the earth in this way. He gave Noah His word on this and God has kept that word. Every time you see a rainbow, you can remember God's promise to us through Noah. It's hard to believe that Noah and his family were the only righteous people living for God on the earth at the time of the flood. It just goes to show you that when you do what is right, God will save you and keep you safe. Do you do what's right so you can have favor and fellowship with God like Noah did? Always do right and trust God no matter what it looks like.

PRAYER:
Dear Lord,
Thank you for saving Noah and his family
And all the animals.
Thank you for the rainbow
To remind us that you love us
And that you will never flood the world again.
Please help me to have favor with you like Noah did.
Keep me and my family safe always, Lord.
In Jesus' name,
AMEN!

DECLARATION:
(say out loud 3 times)

GOD KEEPS ME SAFE

> "Now Israel loved Joseph more than any of his other sons, because he had been born to him in his old age; and he made an ornate robe for him. When his brothers saw that their father loved him more than any of them, they hated him and could not speak a kind word to him."
> Genesis 37:3-4

DID YOU KNOW THAT THE FATHER IN THIS STORY IS A LOT LIKE GOD?

Closeness with God means understanding that no matter what it looks like, He loves all of us the way Joseph's father loved Joseph. God knows us better than we know ourselves. He knows our tendencies and shortcomings and He works to bring about situations to help us become more like His Son, Jesus Christ. Yes, Joseph's father, Israel is like God in this story because just like Joseph's father loved Joseph the most, so does God love US ALL THE MOST. That's right! God loves you, THE MOST and He loves me, THE MOST. God has no favorites. He loves us all with an everlasting love and He wants to shower us with blessings just like Joseph's father did in this passage when he gave Joseph a beautiful (ornate) robe of many colors. Remember too, that when you are in close fellowship with your Heavenly Father, like Joseph was with his father, Israel, others will be jealous. Just like Joseph's brothers were jealous of Joseph's relationship with his Father, Israel, people will also sometimes envy your relationship with the

Lord. When this happens, do what Joseph eventually did in this story and forgive them. Don't hold onto unforgiveness. Forgive, as your Heavenly Father forgives you and remember to pray for them and for yourself.

PRAYER:
Dear Heavenly Father,
Thank you for loving us all the same.
Thank you for showering me with Your love
And for taking care of me.
Forgive me for the times
That I haven't trusted Your love
For me. Help me to know You love me
No matter what!
In Jesus' name,
AMEN!

DECLARATION:
(say out loud 3 times)

I AM CLOSE TO GOD AND HE IS CLOSE TO ME

> **"Now Moses was a humble man, more humble than anyone else on the face of the earth."**
> **Numbers 12:3**

HAVE YOU EVER BEEN AROUND SOMEONE WHO BRAGGED ALL THE TIME?

Closeness with God calls for humility. Humility means that you do not think of yourself higher than you ought to. Humility is knowing that our hope and help come from Jesus and any talent we have was given to us by Him. Moses was very humble. In fact, he couldn't even believe God chose him to lead God's people out of Egypt in the first place and he gave God many excuses as to why God should find someone else. Humility is defined by Merriam-Webster.com as: not proud or haughty; not arrogant or assertive, unpretentious. One of the things God hates is pride. Pride is the opposite of humility. Pride tries to be seen and heard; pride looks at self instead of God. Pride will keep you out of step with the things God is doing. Pride will keep you from a right relationship with God and with others. The Bible is clear that it is God who exalts a person when they are ready for more responsibility. God chose Moses for the major task of going to Pharaoh in Egypt and demanding that Pharaoh let God's people go! In Numbers 12:3 above, we see God describing Moses as the most humble person on the face of the earth. Wow! Humility is definitely important in leading others. Humble leaders and humble people, put others above themselves while still obeying what God told them to do. Remember that it is okay to consider yourself, but others should always be thought of when making your decisions in life.

PRAYER:
Dear Lord,
Thank you for the example You give us in Moses.
Help me to stay humble before You.
Help me to be like Moses.
I want to please You, Lord.
In Jesus' name,
AMEN!

DECLARATION:
(say out loud 3 times)

THE LORD KEEPS ME HUMBLE

> "When there is a prophet among you, I, the Lord, reveal myself to them in visions, I speak to them in dreams. But this is not true of my servant Moses; he is faithful in all my house. With him I speak face to face, clearly and not in riddles; he sees the form of the Lord. Why then were you not afraid to speak against my servant Moses?"
> **Numbers 12:6-8**

IF YOU'RE GOING TO HAVE FELLOWSHIP AND CAMARADERIE WITH GOD, YOU MUST BE FAITHFUL AND BE CAREFUL NOT TO SPEAK AGAINST GOD'S LEADERS.

If you have difficulty with a leader, pray for them, do good to them, don't use them, but go talk to them privately, if needed. Learn the Bible's way for dealing with relationships, never back talk, or slander a leader. God takes this seriously, as we will soon see in this story of Moses, Aaron and Miriam. You may not always agree with your parents, teachers, friends, or leaders at church, but you must find a way to express your frustrations in loving and productive ways without tarnishing people's reputations. God sees and hears and knows all that we say and do and we will give account one day for every idle word that comes out of our mouths. Watch your words and walk in love towards others, especially people who are in authority over you and over others. In chapter 12 of the Book of Numbers, Moses' brother, Aaron and His sister,

Miriam were talking behind Moses' back, like Moses didn't have enough to deal with. Leading almost a million people out of slavery in Egypt through a wilderness with no fast-food restaurant on every corner wasn't easy. The people had a tendency to complain about everything and now, Miriam and Aaron had gone too far. God immediately came down and struck Miriam with a skin disease and Aaron begged Moses to ask God to heal Miriam and forgive them for talking about him behind his back. Moses prays for Miriam, but God doesn't heal her right away. Instead, God puts Miriam outside the camp for seven days before he heals her of leprosy. All of this happened because they spoke against Moses and were ultimately unfaithful to God and to Moses.

PRAYER:
Dearest Lord,
Please forgive me for speaking against others
Especially, those who are in leadership like
My parents, teachers and church people.
I know that if I want to be close to You
I need to put a guard over my mouth
And be a faithful servant like Moses was.
Help me Lord to do these things.
In Jesus' name,
AMEN!

DECLARATION:
(say out loud 3 times)

GOD HELPS ME TO GUARD MY TONGUE

> "From inside the fish Jonah prayed to the Lord his God. He said, 'In my distress I called to the Lord, and he answered me. From deep in the realm of the dead I called for help, and you listened to my cry."
> **Jonah 2:1**

HAVE YOU EVER HEARD THE STORY OF JONAH?

Just like Jonah would soon discover, you're never too far gone that God cannot save you and use you for His glorious purposes. Jonah was the prophet in the Bible that was swallowed by a giant fish and lived to tell about it. Jonah was the guy that disobeyed when God asked Jonah to go to a city called Nineveh to tell the people to change their ways, but instead he went in the OPPOSITE direction to a city known then as Tarshish. God loved the people of Nineveh and wanted to save them from their sins, but Jonah despised the people in that city and so refused to go tell them anything. As the story goes, God sent a giant fish to swallow Jonah and take him to Nineveh AFTER Jonah repents and tells God how sorry he is for disobeying Him. I guess the point I'm making is that even in our rebellion and disobedience, God has a plan for our lives and He expects us to follow that plan and He knows how to keep us in camaraderie with Him. He knew that Jonah just needed some help in obeying God's plan for Nineveh and that's why God sent that fish. I think it's so good of God to send us what we need so that we will come to our senses and not be lost forever. God knows how to keep us in fellowship with Him, even when we are on the run like Jonah and ignoring His directions. Through all of our trials and decisions, God loves us and keeps us by His grace and mercy. We may break fellowship, or camaraderie with God, but He will never leave us, nor forsake us.

PRAYER:
Dear Lord,
Thank you for the example of Jonah in the Bible.
Forgive me, Lord for all the times that I was stubborn, just like Jonah.
Forgive me for disobeying you and for disobeying those who
Are responsible for me. People like my parents, guardians and teachers.
I want to do better Lord. Please help me to hear Your voice
And obey Your voice right away, all the way and in a happy way.
In Your name I pray,
AMEN!

DECLARATION:
(say out loud 3 times)

I HEAR GOD'S VOICE AND I OBEY HIM

> "Alas, Sovereign Lord, I said, I do not know how to speak; I am too young. But the Lord said to me, Do not say, I am too young. You must go to everyone I send you to and say whatever I command you."
> Jeremiah 1:6-7

JEREMIAH WAS JUST A TEENAGER WHEN GOD CALLED HIM TO THE OFFICE OF THE PROPHET.

Just like Jeremiah would soon discover, you're never too young to serve God. The Jewish people were in sin. They had forsaken God by worshiping other gods. The thing about this is that there are no other Gods besides Jesus. He is the way, the truth and the life and no one can get to the Father in heaven, but by Him. I guess the Jewish people of Jeremiah's day had forgotten this and now the only way to really help the Jewish people was to get their attention so they might repent and turn back to God. Sometimes it takes something hard to help us to remember that God is God and He is the Ruler of the world, not us. You can imagine how nervous young Jeremiah was when God told Jeremiah that he would be the guy to go tell the Jewish leaders the bad news, but God helped him and Jeremiah did it. No matter how old or young you are, fellowship and camaraderie with God means obeying his wishes and not making excuses. In the end, God will always give you His Power to do what He asks if you cooperate with Him and trust Him. Even if you get scared, do what He asks and as you go through the motions of obeying Him, He will help you overcome your fear just like He did with the Prophet Jeremiah.

PRAYER:
Dear Lord,
Thank you for the example of Jeremiah.
Thank you for helping Jeremiah overcome his fear
And tell the Jewish people what would happen.
Lord, help me to speak for You.
Help me to go for You and give my all for You.
Help me to never make any excuses, but to follow
Wherever You may lead me.
In Jesus' name,
AMEN!

DECLARATION:
(say out loud 3 times)

I AM NEVER TOO YOUNG OR TOO OLD TO OBEY GOD

> **"Lord Almighty, if you will only look on your servant's misery and remember me, and not forget your servant but give her a son, then I will give him to the Lord for all the days of his life,..."**
> **1 Samuel 1:11**

HANNAH WANTED A SON WITH ALL HER HEART AND IT WAS THROUGH HER, THAT THE PROPHET SAMUEL WAS BORN.

Samuel's mother, Hannah was a godly woman. This means that she loved God and served God all of her life so, when she petitioned the Lord for a son, He answered her. Notice that she made a vow to the Lord and promised to give her son back to God and allow him to serve in the Lord's house all of his life. If you know anything about Samuel, he was a mighty man of God who served God all of his life. Samuel did many great things in God's name and he remained faithful to God all his days. His mother Hannah was faithful in keeping her word to God and this faithfulness was in her son, Samuel, too. Camaraderie in Christ, often starts with our parents' example in training us up to serve the Lord. Hannah was true to her word. When Samuel was born, she brought him to the temple for training as soon as he was old enough and Eli, the Priest, taught Samuel how to minister in the House of God. This is what parents, or guardians are called to do. The wonderful thing about God is that He knows that not all parents are serving Him like they should, but we are still called to honor our father and our mother and God is faithful to give us spiritual parents to help guide us. People like, aunts, uncles, cousins, friends, grandparents, pastors, teachers and church leaders. Keep your vows to the Lord like Hannah did and your faithfulness will affect future generations.

PRAYER:
Dearest Lord,
Thank you for the example of Hannah and Samuel in the Bible.
Please help me to be like them. Help me to be faithful to You.
Help me to keep my promises to You and to others.
In Jesus' name,
AMEN!

DECLARATION:
(say out loud 3 times)

I KEEP MY PROMISES TO GOD AND TO OTHERS

> "So the king gave the order, and they brought Daniel and threw him into the lion's den. The king said to Daniel, 'May your God, whom you serve continually, rescue you!'"
> **Daniel 6:16**

DANIEL WAS A WISE MAN WHO LOVED GOD SO MUCH THAT WHEN A LAW WAS MADE TELLING DANIEL HE COULD NO LONGER PRAY TO HIS GOD, DANIEL CONTINUED TO DO SO ANYWAY AND WAS THEREFORE THROWN INTO A LION'S DEN WHERE VERY HUNGRY LIONS WERE WAITING.

The story goes on to show that God miraculously spared Daniel by shutting the mouths of the lions all night long. Daniel, with God's help, was kept safe and because of Daniel's strong character and God's great power, King Darius issued a decree that you can read for yourself here in Daniel 6:25-28: "Then King Darius wrote to all the nations and peoples of every language in all the earth: May you prosper greatly! I issue a decree that in every part of my kingdom people must fear and reverence the God of Daniel. For he is the living God and he endures forever; his kingdom will not be destroyed, his dominion will never end. He rescues and he saves; he performs signs and wonders in the heavens and on the earth. He has rescued Daniel from the power of the lions." WOW! The entire Persian Empire became believers in Jesus Christ in one day because of Daniel's example of bravery.

PRAYER:
Dearest Lord Jesus,
Thank you for the example of Daniel in the lion's den.
Thank you for his wisdom and bravery.
Help me Lord to be like Daniel.
Help me to trust You no matter what.
Help me to stand up against things that I know
Go against Your truth in the Bible.
In Jesus' name,
AMEN!

DECLARATION:
(say out loud 3 times)

I DO WHAT IS RIGHT

> "Then Esther sent this reply to Mordecai: 'Go gather together all the Jews who are in Susa, and fast for me. Do not eat or drink for three days, night or day. I and my attendants will fast as you do. When this is done, I will go to the king, even though it is against the law. And if I perish, I perish.'"
> Esther 4:15-16)

ESTHER WAS A YOUNG JEWISH GIRL WHO WAS RAISED BY HER COUSIN, MORDECAI AFTER THE DEATH OF HER PARENTS.

The King of Persia, whose name was Xerxes, needed a new queen and so he had his men round up all the young maidens to be brought to his palace to see which he would choose to be his new queen. Mordecai worked at the palace but refused to bow down to a proud man named Haman. Mordecai, as a Jew knew that he was to only bow to the one, true God, the God of the Bible. Haman was enraged and set about making a plan to do away with Mordecai and all of the Jews in Persia. Things became so bad that after Esther was made Queen of Persia, she had to make a decision to go to her husband, King Xerxes without first being summoned. Going before the king unannounced was against Persian law and could result in death, but Esther had been given favor with King Xerxes. He loved Esther very much and held out his royal scepter to her, granting her permission to speak and not be put to death. Eventually, Esther was able to reveal the plot of Haman against her people and all the Jews in Persia were saved because of Esther's bravery and the sovereignty of God in allowing her to rise to be the Queen of Persia.

PRAYER:

Dear Father in Heaven,
Thank you for the bravery of Queen Esther.
Thank you for saving the Jewish people through her.
Thank you that we are granted the power of prayer to seek You when things get hard.
Thank you that no matter what, Your Word is higher than any law made by people.
Help me Lord to be brave like Esther and Mordecai.
No matter what I face, help me to stand for justice.
In Jesus' name,
AMEN!

DECLARATION:
(say out loud 3 times)

I AM BRAVE LIKE ESTHER AND MORDECAI

> "But Ruth replied, 'Don't urge me to leave you or to turn back from you. Where you go I will go, and where you stay I will stay. Your people will be my people and your God my God."
> Ruth 1:16

RUTH WAS FAITHFUL TO HER MOTHER-IN-LAW, NAOMI.

Ruth and Orpah were married to Naomi's two sons who died. Naomi's husband also died so that all three women were widowed. Naomi told Ruth and Orpah to return to their homes in other places because she had nothing left to offer them. Orpah kissed and hugged Naomi and left in tears, but Ruth CLUNG to Naomi and said that no matter what, she would never, ever leave her. Ruth stayed with Naomi and took care of her all of her life and Ruth went on to marry a well to do man named Boaz. Ruth became the great grandmother of King David, and it is through the lineage of King David that JESUS, THE MESSIAH WAS BORN! Ruth is a beautiful picture of how the Lord wants His people to cling to Him, to be faithful to Him even when others aren't. God took care of Ruth and Naomi in their time of need and used Ruth to help bring forth the lineage of Jesus Christ. Simple faithfulness to God brings BIG RETURNS, but you need to stay committed all your life. You need to cling to the Lord and do what He needs you to do for His kingdom and His glory.

PRAYER:
Dear God,
Thank you for the example of Ruth in the Bible.
Thank you that she never left the person who loved her
And needed her help.
We need to be like Ruth, too.
We need to hold on to You, Lord.
Help us to hold on to You and never let You go.
In Jesus' name,
AMEN!

DECLARATION:
(say out loud 3 times)

I HOLD ON TO JESUS

> "As he neared Damascus on his journey, suddenly a light from heaven flashed around him. He fell to the ground and heard a voice say to him, 'Saul, Saul, why do you persecute me?'"
> Acts 9:3-4

HAVE YOU HEARD ABOUT THE APOSTLE PAUL (WHOSE NAME WAS SAUL BEFORE GOD CHANGED IT TO PAUL) IN THE BIBLE?

Paul is the man God called to the task of writing most of the New Testament. He was a very intelligent, Jewish leader in his day and at first, he did NOT believe in Jesus. In fact, at the time of this story from Acts chapter 9, Paul was traveling to a city called Damascus to hurt Christians and put them in jail. Paul thought that Christians were wrong for believing that Jesus was the Messiah of the world and on the way to Damascus, Jesus showed Paul (Saul) the truth. Jesus spoke to Paul from a bright light and in a loud voice told Paul that He, Jesus was the Messiah, the Holy One of Israel. Paul instantly believed and his life was never the same after that. You see, until Paul understood that Jesus was high and lifted up, Paul couldn't serve Jesus. It's very important to know your place. You need to understand that God's ways are not our ways. God's thoughts are not our thoughts. He is King of all and He will and must be exalted in your life. Once Paul understood this, He could serve Jesus with his whole heart. Paul went on to suffer much for preaching about Jesus, but He counted everything as loss for the sake of knowing Christ. Are you like this? Have you surrendered to the Lordship of Jesus? Is He lifted up in your life? A servant is never above his master. That would be like your dog calling all the shots in your life and telling you what to do. A dog doesn't have that authority and neither do we. Jesus should govern our lives and when we let him lead us, things always work out for the best.

PRAYER:
Dear Jesus,
Thank you for the cross.
Thank you for the Apostle Paul.
Thank you for the Bible that teaches me how to live Your way.
Help me to put You first in my life.
Help me to see You high and lifted up.
In Your name I pray,
AMEN!

DECLARATION:
(say out loud 3 times)

JESUS IS HIGH AND LIFTED UP

"But Jesus often withdrew to lonely places and prayed."
Luke 5:16

EVEN JESUS NEEDED GOD TO COMPLETE HIS MISSION.

All of us have a mission from God and we need to know God and spend time with God in prayer so that we can get the strength and the wisdom to complete our tasks and ultimate mission for Him. Jesus would often retreat to places where there were no people so that He could pray and talk to His Heavenly Father. Developing your prayer life by setting aside time each day to read scripture and pray, is very important to staying connected to God. My prayer is that this devotional book will be a part of your daily time with the Lord so that you will stay close to Him all of your life. Set a time to meet with God each day and try your best to remain faithful to that time with Him. Keep a journal of things that come to your mind in prayer. Underline any scripture in your Bible that may catch your attention. Don't be afraid to write in your Bible when God shows you something important and take that scripture that you underlined and say it out loud to yourself several times. Think about it, pray it out loud and hide it in your memory and in your heart. Write it down if you have time. Writing it out in your own words can help you remember it better, too. God's Word is more precious than silver, diamonds and gold. Treasure His Word. It will guide you and help you. God's Word will never pass away. It is eternal and very powerful indeed.

PRAYER:
Dear God,
Please help me to set aside time each day to meet with you.
Help me to read and memorize scriptures in the Bible.
Help me to keep a journal and to try my best
To meet with you each day.
Help me, Lord to be faithful to attend church,
Youth group and conferences and camps to help me grow in my faith.
Whatever happens, please let me never give up but keep trying.
I ask it all in Your name,
AMEN!

DECLARATION:
(say out loud 3 times)

I MEET WITH GOD EACH DAY TO STUDY HIS WORD AND PRAY

CAMARADERIE WITH OTHERS:
"Do nothing out of selfish ambition or vain conceit. Rather, in humility value others above yourselves, not looking to your own interests but each of you to the interests of the others."
Philippians 2:3-4

NOTES

> "In your relationships with one another, have the same mindset as Christ Jesus: Who, being in very nature God, did not consider equality with God something to be used to his own advantage; rather, he made himself nothing by taking the very nature of a servant, being made in human likeness."
> Philippians 2:5-7

JESUS WAS GOD AND MAN AT THE SAME TIME.

Jesus left the splendor of Heaven to come to earth as a little baby and grow up to take our place and die on the cross for our sins. He was the strongest, the greatest, the best, He was God! Yet, He humbled Himself for us. He became a person in order to save those who would believe in His sacrifice. If Jesus can leave all of that wonderful splendor and glory in Heaven to come and become a mere human for us, then we can humble ourselves too and not think only of ourselves. If Jesus wanted to, He could have stayed with His Father in Heaven instead of suffering here on earth for us. Jesus chose to serve us in this way because He knew that there was no other way to save us from the penalty of sin which is eternal separation from God. In your relationships with others, be like Christ who humbled Himself so that we could be raised up with Him.

PRAYER:
Dear Lord,
Forgive me when I act selfishly.
Forgive me when I don't stop to consider other people's feelings.
You were God and yet, You came to earth to become human for us.
Thank you for the cross. Thank you for Your sacrifice for my sins.
Please help me to serve others like you did.
In Your name I pray,
AMEN!

DECLARATION:
(say out loud 3 times)

I SERVE OTHERS LIKE JESUS DID

> **"Do everything without grumbling or arguing, so that you may become blameless and pure, children of God without fault in a warped and crooked generation. Then you will shine among them like stars in the sky."**
> **Philippians 2:14-15**

WHEN I WAS A YOUNG CHILD, OUR LARGE FAMILY OF SIX WOULD TRAVEL LONG DISTANCES IN OUR BIG, LIGHT BLUE STATION WAGON.

I don't think they even make Station Wagon cars anymore, but my father and mother would sit up front on these long trips and do whatever they could to keep their four children from growing restless. Like any family on a long trip, arguments and complaints inevitably would ensue, but when these moments of tension occurred, my father would put some music on the radio that we all knew and loved. Before long, the six of us would be singing together at the top of our lungs, having forgotten all about whatever it was that was concerning us a moment ago. I can still picture it all like it was yesterday. Those were good times, but they may not have been so great if we had not learned how to get along. Life is hard sometimes and people get hungry and cranky. People can forget to be forgiving or loving and instead act selfishly which can cause hard feelings. If we are going to shine for Jesus in this world, we need to learn to keep happy hearts towards ourselves and others.

PRAYER:
Dearest Lord,
Please forgive me when I argue with others
Or complain and demand my own way.
Help me Lord to sing unto You.
Help me to keep my heart happy towards
You, myself and others.
In Jesus' name,
AMEN!

DECLARATION:
(say out loud 3 times)

I DO EVERYTHING WITHOUT ARGUING AND COMPLAINING

> **"Therefore encourage one another and build each other up, just as in fact you are doing."**
> **1 Thessalonians 5:11**

DO YOU REMEMBER BUILDING TALL TOWERS WITH BLOCKS WHEN YOU WERE A KID?

Maybe you work with children and have watched them build towers with their blocks. If you have kids of your own either now, or someday, chances are block towers are things you have seen before. Children love to see how high they can build a tower of blocks before the tower tips over. I remember when I was a preschool teacher, there were always those kids who'd go around the classroom during play time and knock over other people's blocks. Inevitably, there would be lots of tears from the child whose tower was destroyed. I think this block tower analogy is good to remember when dealing with people of all ages. God tells us to build one another up, not push one another down. Imagine people like fragile towers that can easily be pushed over. Now, imagine a group of people working together to build a strong tower that they all can look at and enjoy. This is God's way.

PRAYER:
Dear Lord,
Please help me to build others up
And not cut them down.
Help me to build strong relationships.
Help me to be like You, Lord.
I ask it all in Your name,
AMEN!

DECLARATION:
(say out loud 3 times)

I BUILD OTHERS UP

Two are better than one, because they have a good return for their labor: If either of them falls down, one can help the other up. But pity anyone who falls and has no one to help them up.
Ecclesiastes 4:9-10

WHEN I WAS YOUNG, I LOVED BEING IN A POPULAR SCOUT GROUP.

We'd sell cookies, go to Scout Meetings with our friends and earn badges to put on our sashes. I remember traveling by bus to Washington, D.C. with my Scout Troop and singing songs about finding peanuts and Noah's Ark, but my all-time favorite thing we ever did was go camping in the rain. I'm sure the adults who had to take care of us didn't think it was all that great, but most of us who were there thought it was exciting. The rain would pelt the top of the tent and we'd scream. I think we drove all the troop leaders and den mothers crazy with our silliness, not to mention the isolation of having to stay inside a tent with eight other girls until the rain stopped. At first it was fun, but after a while the sun started going down and we were all freezing cold. I think I remember the eight of us scrunching our sleeping bags together to keep warm so that we could finally fall asleep. That's what being in the kingdom of God is like. You're better and stronger together. We are a team. Team Jesus!

PRAYER:
Dear Lord,
Thank you that I don't have to do life alone.
Thank you that I have friends in Christ who help me.
Please help me to stay strong in You
And together with my brothers and sisters in Christ.
In Jesus' name I pray,
AMEN!

DECLARATION:
(say out loud 3 times)

I HAVE FRIENDS TO HELP ME

> **"Make sure that nobody pays back wrong for wrong, but always strive to do what is good for each other and for everyone else."**
> **1 Thessalonians 5:15**

HAVE YOUR EVER HEARD OF A SACRIFICE BUNT IN THE GAME OF BASEBALL?

Sometimes when a baseball player is batting, their coach will give them a signal to BUNT THE BALL! This means that they are to lightly tap the ball with their bat as the ball is coming to them. If done correctly, they will cause the runner on first to advance to second, but they will most likely be thrown out at first. This is why bunting is a sacrifice. You get out so that your teammate can advance. As you probably know, the team with the most runs in baseball after nine innings is the WINNER! All the players win. Not just one player. All of them! This is like the kingdom of God. We must work together so that everybody wins. This means sacrifice and it also means continuing to work together even when each member of the team makes mistakes. Everyone will fail sometimes, but it is up to us as teammates to continue to encourage one another and help TEAM JESUS to WIN, WIN, WIN! GO TEAM!! GO TEAM JESUS!!

PRAYER:
Dear Lord,
Thank you that I'm part of Your Team.
Thank you that all believers in Jesus get to play one
Your Team forever.
Help me and help us all to be good sports.
Help us to do our part so that everyone on
Your Team will WIN!
In Jesus' name I pray,
AMEN!

DECLARATION:
(say out loud 3 times)

I AM A WINNER WITH JESUS

> "Now we ask you, brothers and sisters, to acknowledge those who work hard among you, who care for you in the Lord and who admonish you. Hold them in the highest regard in love because of their work. Live in peace with each other."
> 1 Thessalonians 5:12-13

THINK ABOUT ALL OF THE PEOPLE THAT HELP YOU GROW AND LEARN.

Think about your parents, guardians, family members, church leaders, coaches and teachers. Think too, about all the people who have helped you along the way. Maybe the person who showed you how to tie your shoe, write your name, throw a baseball, cook a meal, sew on a button, or how to read. The person who teaches you the Bible, or how to drive a car, or open a bank account. Anyone who has cared for you and has instructed you or taught you right from wrong is to be held in the highest regard. This means that you are to treat kindly and with thanksgiving, those who have shared their time and energy with you. Then, you go out and do the same for others.

PRAYER:

Dearest Lord,

Thank you for all the people who have helped me in my life.

Thank you for all the people who will help me in the future.

I'm asking you to bless the people who have helped me grow.

Bless their families and lives and keep them safe.

Help us all to live together in love, unity and peace.

In Jesus' name,

AMEN!

DECLARATION:
(say out loud 3 times)

I AM THANKFUL FOR THOSE WHO HELP ME

> "Therefore, as we have opportunity, let us do good to all people, especially to those who belong to the family of believers."
> **Galatians 6:10**

HAVE YOU EVER HEARD THE SAYING THAT IF YOU CAN'T SAY OR DO SOMETHING NICE, THEN SAY OR DO NOTHING AT ALL?

When I was a child, my mother would say this to me and my siblings quite often and when I became a Christian I was surprised to find that this idea is found in the Bible. God wishes for us to do good and speak well of all people or SAY NOTHING. Sometimes it is best to say nothing at all, especially if you are upset. It is better to walk away and get calm before reacting and then doing or saying something that you will regret. This is especially true in the family of God. We are to be kind and gentle with one another who serve the Lord knowing that it is not always an easy task to follow Jesus. Believers in Jesus are family whether you like it or not. We are family and we are to find ways to get along and work out our differences by talking them through and finding constructive ways to fix problems that arise. All families fight, but when they do, they can work through their differences in ways that help everyone in God's family.

PRAYER:
Dear Heavenly Father,
Thank you that I'm in the family of God.
Thank you for all of my brothers and sisters in Christ.
Help me to do my part to walk in unity and love with
My brothers and sisters in the Lord.
Help us all in the Kingdom of God to remember
To say nothing and do nothing unless it will help
Others and not hurt them.
I'm asking for You to help me and all of the believers
In the world to accomplish this together.
I ask it all in Your name,
AMEN!

DECLARATION:
(say out loud 3 times)

I DO GOOD TO ALL PEOPLE, ESPECIALLY THOSE
WHO BELIEVE IN JESUS

> "May the Lord show mercy to the household of Onesiphorus, because he often refreshed me and was not ashamed of my chains. On the contrary, when he was in Rome, he searched hard for me until he found me."
> 2 Timothy 1:16-17

WHEN PAUL NEEDED A FRIEND, A MAN NAMED ONESIPHORUS WAS THERE FOR HIM.

When Paul needed to feel better after being put in chains for preaching the gospel, Onesiphorus took care of him. It says that Onesiphorus even searched hard for Paul until he found Paul and made sure that Paul was okay. This reminds me of the story of the Good Samaritan found in the Book of Luke in the Bible. A traveler is suffering on the side of the road and several people just pass him by refusing to help him. Then, a man known as a Samaritan stops to help the hurt traveler. Samaritan's were not popular at the time of Jesus when this story was told, but it reminds me of how Onesiphorus did whatever necessary to help his friend, the Apostle Paul. As followers of Jesus, we should be like Onesiphorus and the Good Samaritan, even if others aren't. We shouldn't walk by people who need help and not help them if it is in our power to do so. We can't help everyone, but we can always do something, even if all we do is pray.

PRAYER:
Dear Lord,
There are hurting people everywhere.
Help me, as Your Follower, to assist others when I am able.
Keep me safe from harm as I reach out to others.
Help me to use wisdom in helping others and ask for help
From older people that know more than I do.
I pray right now for all of the hurting people in the world.
In Jesus' name,
AMEN!

DECLARATION:
(say out loud 3 times)

I HELP OTHERS WHEN I CAN AND I ASK FOR HELP WHEN I NEED TO

> "There are six things the Lord hates, seven that are detestable to him: haughty eyes, a lying tongue, hands that shed innocent blood, a heart that devises wicked schemes, feet that are quick to rush into evil, a false witness who pours out lies and a person who stirs up conflict in the community."
> Proverbs 6:16-19

THE LORD LOVES PEOPLE, BUT HE DOESN'T ALWAYS LOVE WHAT THEY DO.

There are things that God really hates because He knows that if you do them, you could lose your way and be lost from Him. Just like a child must stay close to its mother while in the grocery story or risk being lost, so staying away from the things God hates, can keep you close to Him all your life. He doesn't want to lose you. When you were a small child, do you remember your parents telling you to hold their hand while crossing the street? They probably told you not to touch a hot stove, or not to play with matches because you could start a fire. I'm sure they told you to wash your hands and take a bath, or shower to keep you healthy from too many germs. Every house has rules to follow and so does God's house. Just like any good parent, God gives us rules to live by so that we will stay safe. In His Word, the Bible, He is clear what He wants and what He doesn't want for His children. If you're not sure what God likes, look it up in the Bible, ask your pastor or youth leader. Always wait to do something until you're sure it's okay. This will keep you safe and happy.

PRAYER:
Dear Jesus,
I know that there are things that You don't approve of.
I know that Your ways are not the world's way.
Help me to know Your ways, Lord.
Help me to love what You love and
To hate what You hate.
I know that You love all people, but You are God
And You decide what is good and right, not us.
Help me to not be wise in my own eyes, but to come to You
And to trusted church leaders, parents and friends for help.
In Jesus' name,
AMEN!

DECLARATION:
(say out loud 3 times)

I LOVE WHAT GOD SAYS IS GOOD

> "Your word is a lamp for my feet, a light for my path."
> Psalm 119:105

HAVE YOU EVER GONE CAMPING AND NEEDED TO WALK IN THE DARK?

Like most good campers, you would use a flashlight, or your cell phone light to illuminate the way in front of you so that you can see. Without the flashlight, you'd probably trip and fall, or even worse, lose your way in the dark. This is like God's Law, the Bible. If you're going to find your way in this world, especially in relationships, you're going to need to see which way to go. God's Word, the Bible has something to say about everything you'll need to see in this world. No matter what you're facing, the Bible can show you the way. The way to turn on the light of the Bible is simply to open it up and read it. There's even something called a "Concordance" in the back of most Bible's that can help you look up topics you need help in. Things like fear, anger, grace, mercy, money, people, relationships and so much more. Let the light and lamp of God's Word light up your path.

PRAYER:
Dear Lord,
Thank you for leaving the Bible here for us.
I know that Your Word, the Bible can help me in my relationships with others.
I know that the Bible is a lamp for my feet and a light for my path.
Help me to always go to Your Word, the Holy Bible for instruction and help.
In Jesus' name,
AMEN!

DECLARATION:
(say out loud 3 times)

THE BIBLE HELPS ME TO SEE IN THE DARK

> **"All Scripture is God-breathed and is useful for teaching, rebuking, correcting and training in righteousness, so that the servant of God may be thoroughly equipped for every good work."**
> **2 Timothy 3:16**

DO YOU KNOW WHAT THE BIBLE IS?

The Bible is God's history book. The Bible is God's story of how it all began and how He would one day send His Son, Jesus into the world to save us from our sins. The Bible is God's instructional manual for life. He left it here for us to know Him and to know what He wants for us. It's His storybook that He wants you to read and memorize and hide in your heart so that you'll know Him better and you'll know what to do in this world. You can trust the Bible. God spoke to people of old by His Holy Spirit and told them what to write. God gave Moses the 10 Commandments so that His people would know what is right and what is wrong. Thirty-five different people wrote the Bible over the course of thousands of years, yet both the Old Testament and New Testament connect and work together. Like a literary quilt, God patched the pieces of the Bible together over the course of many centuries to produce a manuscript for living life His way. The Bible also has over 300 prophecies written within it and many have already come to pass. The Bible says that not one jot or tittle in the Bible will pass away until all the prophecies have come to pass.

The Bible also says that heaven and earth will pass away, but God's Word, the Bible will remain FOREVER! Wow! God's Word is eternal. Trust it. Know it. Read it. Study it. Live it. Tell others about it. Let it teach you, correct you and train you so that you are ready for whatever comes your way.

PRAYER:
Dear Heavenly Father,
Your Word, the Bible is true no matter what the world may say.
Your Word is able to make me wise and help me to know what is right and wrong.
Lord, help me to know Your Word and to share it with others.
In Jesus' name,
AMEN!

DECLARATION:
(say out loud 3 times)

THE BIBLE CAME FROM GOD

> **"The tongue has the power of life and death, and those who love it will eat its fruit."**
> **Proverbs 18:21**

HAVE YOU EVER HEARD THAT OLD SAYING: STICKS AND STONES MAY BREAK MY BONES, BUT NAMES WILL NEVER HURT ME?

This statement is not true and Proverbs 18:21 confirms it. Words have power. When God spoke, "Let there be light and there was light," we see the power of words. God's kingdom is a kingdom of words. The Bible tells us that we can have what we say. This is sometimes called a self-fulfilling prophecy. Whatever words we speak over ourselves or over others, can cause power for it to happen. Do you remember a time when someone said something mean or hurtful to you? How did it make you feel? Do you still think about those words they spoke? Even if someone says they are sorry for saying hurtful things, those words can still be in the back of our minds. If this is you, do what it says in the Bible and cast down those bad thoughts. Take them captive and break their power in the name of Jesus. Words can bring good or bad, life or death, but the name of Jesus is always more powerful than anything. Use the Lord's name to break those word curses over yourself and others.

PRAYER:
Dear Lord,
Help me to speak life over myself and others.
Help me to say good things or say nothing at all.
I ask in Your name that all word curses in my life be broken right now.
I declare that any negative words spoken to me and about me that were not life giving
Fall to the ground and die.
Any words that I have spoken over others that were not life giving
I break now in the name of Jesus!
AMEN!

DECLARATION:
(say out loud 3 times)

I SPEAK LIFE GIVING WORDS OVER MYSELF AND OTHERS

**"Then Peter came to Jesus and asked, 'Lord, how many times shall I forgive my brother or sister who sins against me? Up to seven times?' Jesus answered, 'I tell you, not seven times, but seventy times seven."
Matthew 18:21-22**

FORGIVENESS IS A BIG PART OF GOD'S KINGDOM!

Do you know how much seventy times seven is? It multiplies out to four hundred and ninety!! WOW! That's a lot of forgiveness, but nevertheless, that's what God's Word says here in the eighteenth chapter of Matthew. He tells us in other places in the Bible too that if we want God to forgive our sins, we must forgive others of their sins. Forgive and you shall be forgiven. That's the way it works. A lot of times we want to pick and choose who to forgive because we think that some sins are worse than others, but it doesn't work this way. God is the judge, not us. He will judge each person because He is the one who knows each heart. Our job is to forgive, but this can be very hard. I remember a person I had a hard time forgiving. This person hurt me a lot and so I was angry and refused to talk to him for a long time, but one day God showed me something. He showed me that this person was just like a little child to him. The Lord showed me a vision of this person playing ball and he was just a little boy with loads of light shining all around him. I heard the Lord say, "This is how I see him." After that, I went home and called this person on the phone and asked them to forgive me for holding onto my anger and unforgiveness. This is what we are called to do. Let go of our anger and forgive. God will help you. Just ask Him.

PRAYER:
Dearest Lord and Savior,
Please forgive me for holding onto my anger and walking in unforgiveness towards others.
I pray that I will remember that You are the judge, not me.
I pray that You will help me to always walk in forgiveness
Even if that means seventy times seven times.
In Jesus' name I pray,
AMEN!

DECLARATION:
(say out loud 3 times)

I FORGIVE AND AM FORGIVEN

PASTOR KAREN'S TESTIMONY:

Why I Became A Believer

When I was roughly 30 years old, I became fearful of dying. At the time, I was happily married with a 1 year old son and I was living what I thought was my best life. It made no sense that I suddenly developed this irrational fear of death and dying. Some tried to blame it on the fact that I was a new mother, however, I knew that it was so much more than that. My husband had a very good job; we lived in a beautiful home in a wonderful community with great schools. I had no worries. In fact, I would say that those years were probably some of the best years of my life, but I continued to experience irrational fear and torment on a weekly, sometimes daily basis. I remember becoming so desperate to feel at peace, that I began inviting visitors into my home when they would stop by to do their evangelizing. Now, I want you to be sure to ALWAYS check with your parent or guardian before letting anyone you don't know into your home, but, for me, it was through these several visitors to my home that I was given my first glimpse of hope. God can use anyone, or anything to help us see the light and that is what He did for me. I remember being taken to Ephesians chapter 6:12 in the Bible and reading these words:

"For our struggle is not against flesh and blood, but against the rulers, against the authorities, against the powers of the dark world and against the spiritual forces of evil in the heavenly realms."

My visitors explained to me that what I was experiencing was a spiritual battle. They began to help me see that there was so much more than just the physical world and the more they shared, the more the spiritual light bulbs went on. What they told me is exactly what was happening. I couldn't believe it. I felt like they were the only people on planet earth who understood what I was going through. The battle was very real and I could feel it and now I was being given tools to defeat it.

This battle went on for two more months and each time that spirit of fear tried to come to torment me I would stand against it. I had learned that the Word of God, the Bible, is a sword in the spirit realm and just like Jesus used the Word of God to defeat Satan in the wilderness in Matthew chapter 4, I too would have to learn to use the Word of God.

Each time I began to feel afraid, I would remind Satan of 2 Timothy 1:7 which says:

"For the Spirit God gave us does not make us timid, but gives us power, love and self-discipline."

In some versions of the Bible, the word "fear" is used instead of the word, "timid." Either way, you get the idea. The idea is to take your sword and defeat the thing you're facing and don't back down until you overcome it.

I'm happy to say that after two long months of dealing with that fear, it finally broke. I woke up one morning and it had left. I could feel that it was gone and it's never coming back. What the devil meant for harm, the Lord will use for good. All that this trial did was make me stronger and it taught me how to fight spiritually and in the supernatural realm.

Since my conversion and difficulty all of those years ago, I have had three more children, completed seminary training, become a licensed minister and started my own ministry to help young people and families learn about Jesus Christ. I have also experienced much adversity being a woman in ministry and much difficulty in my personal life, but through it all, the Lord was with me. He never left me and He has shown me that the best is yet to come. I pray you know the Savior, too. I pray that you receive Him for yourself so that you too, can know the joy of His presence no matter what happens in your life. He never promised that we wouldn't have trouble, but He did say that He would never leave us, nor forsake us and that He would be with us even to the end of the age.

HOW TO BECOME A CHRISTIAN:

1. BELIEVE IN JESUS CHRIST:

**"If you declare with your mouth, 'Jesus is Lord,' and believe in your heart that God raised him from the dead, you will be saved. For it is with your heart that you believe and are justified, and it is with your mouth that you profess your faith and are saved."
Romans 10:9-10**

**"For God so loved the world that he gave his one and only Son, that whoever believes in him shall not perish but have eternal life."
Romans 3:23**

To be saved from eternal separation from God you must put your faith in His only begotten (meaning He came from God) Son, Jesus Christ. You must believe this in your heart and confess it with your mouth. Trusting, relying and believing in Christ Jesus is essential to experiencing salvation. Salvation is knowing that Jesus paid the price to save you from eternal separation from God.

---

2. WHAT DO WE NEED TO BE SAVED FROM?

"For all have sinned and fall short of the glory of God."
Romans 3:23

"For the wages of sin is death, but the gift of God is eternal life in Christ Jesus our Lord."
Romans 6:23

The first man, Adam and the first woman, Eve disobeyed God. They broke God's command to leave alone the tree in the middle of the Garden of Eden where they were both living. Jesus needs to be in the middle of our hearts and in the middle of all we say and do. The entire garden was theirs, but they took what wasn't theirs to take and so they went from being perfect and without sin, to sinful people. Because of this original sin, we are all born sinners, just like Adam and Eve. The problem is that sin keeps us from God. Sin has a cost and the cost is spiritual death. We had to be saved from our sins.

---

3. CONFESS YOUR SINS AND BE SAVED:

"If we confess our sins, he is faithful and just and will forgive us our sins and purify us from all unrighteousness." 1 John 1:9

"No temptation has overtaken you except what is common to mankind. And God is faithful; he

will not let you be tempted beyond what you can bear. But when you are tempted, he will also provide a way out so that you can endure it."
1 Corinthians 10:13

Each night before you go to bed, check in with God and confess any sin in your life. Confess any sin that you remember committing. Ask God to show you if there is something you need to confess to Him. This will keep your life pure before God. Also, throughout the day, if you do something that you know is a sin, quickly repent and tell God you're sorry. Repent means to turn from it, to stop and turn from what you're doing.

Everyone is tempted by his, or her own desires. There are weaknesses in all of us, but we must give them to God and ask Him to help us to live free from our own selfish desires. The Bible says that the spirit man inside of us is willing, but the flesh is weak, however, God will make a way of escape so that you are able to see how to turn from what you're doing. Turning from sin is very important. You must do this as an act of your own free will. God will not make you. He will help you. He will do it with you, but you must cooperate with His Holy Spirit and listen for His leading. That small still voice inside of you that tells you right from wrong is God's voice speaking. The world calls it your conscience, but it's God's Spirit living on the inside of you.

4. WE ARE SAVED BY GRACE NOT WORKS:

"For it is by grace you have been saved, through faith - and this is not from yourselves, it is the gift of God - not by works, so that no one can boast." Ephesians 2:8-9

**"All of us have become like one who is unclean, and our righteous acts are like filthy rags; we all shrivel up like a leaf, and like the wind our sins sweep us away."
Isaiah 64:6**

This idea of being saved by grace is very important. The word, "GRACE," means getting something we don't deserve. We don't deserve to be saved. We don't deserve God's mercy, but He gives it because He is good and He loves us and wishes for all people to come to repentance and be saved. You cannot do anything to earn God's love.

---

5. WHY IS SIN SUCH A BIG DEAL?

"Because through Christ Jesus the law of the Spirit who gives life has set you free from the law of sin and death." Romans 8:2

**"Let us approach God's throne of grace with confidence, so that we may receive mercy and find grace to help us in our time of need."
Hebrews 4:16**

"In fact, the law requires that nearly everything be cleansed with blood, and without the shedding of blood there is no forgiveness." Hebrew 9:22

Before Adam and Eve sinned, they were without sin. They were perfect. When sin entered so did the penalty of sin which is eternal death. God sent Jesus to pay for our sins. The righteous requirement was perfection. Jesus was the only perfect person to ever live on earth after the fall of Adam and Eve. Jesus lived a sinless life so He could break the curse of sin, hell and eternal death.

When you sin, you give the devil LEGAL RIGHT to attack you, your family and all that concerns you. This is why you must go to God daily and ask Him to forgive you. Ask Him to apply the blood to your sin because without the blood of Jesus there would be NO FORGIVENESS for you. This is because there is LIFE in the BLOOD of Jesus. You need to apply LIGHT to those dark places. After this, ask the Lord to apply His resurrection power to your situation. Go boldly to the throne room of heaven to ask for forgiveness. Apply the blood of Jesus and then apply His resurrection power so that you can go forward in His power and do well for Him.

You will always make mistakes, but you can conquer sin every day and stay covered under the protection of the cross if you apply the blood of Jesus and His resurrection power. Remember: don't give legal access to the devil by continuing to live in sin.

A PRAYER TO RECEIVE JESUS:

Dear Lord,
Please forgive me of all my sins.
I'm so sorry for sinning against You.
I know that you are the Son of God.
I believe it in my heart
and I confess it with my mouth.
Jesus, You are Lord of all Creation.
I believe in the resurrection.
I believe that You conquered death.
I believe that you died on the cross
For my sins and for the sins
Of the whole world.
Please save me, Lord.
I want to live with You in heaven
And I want to live for You on earth.
Make me a child of the King,
King Jesus.
Please write my name in Your Book,
The Lamb's Book of Life.
Help me to live for You Lord.
Help me to die to myself
And become all you want me to be.
Help me find a church family.
Help me to read and understand my Bible
and be water baptized to show the world

<u>That I belong to You.
I ask this all in Your name, Jesus!
AMEN!</u>

<u>If you prayed that prayer, I want you to contact me.
I want to help you grow in your faith.
Contact information is on the next page.</u>

If you prayed the prayer of Salvation to receive Jesus as your Savior on the page before this one, I want to hear from you. I want to help you grow. Being a Christian is all about growing. You can't stay the same. There's so much to learn. Let us at NOW Ministries, Inc. help you. May God bless you and keep you in faith, hope and love. May you run to win and never give up knowing this, that the trying of your faith builds patience and a perfect work of God within you. AMEN!

CONTACT INFORMATION

NOW MINISTRIES, INC.
Pastor Karen Fitzpatrick
P.O. Box 9803
Chesapeake, VA 23321

PHONE:
757-618-0777

FACEBOOK:
@goforthNOW

INSTAGRAM:
nowpowerva

WEBSITE:
nowministriesinc.com

THE TEN COMMANDMENTS
Exodus 20:1-17

I. LOVE GOD

II. DO NOT WORSHIP IDOLS

III. DO NOT USE THE LORD'S NAME IN VAIN

IV. KEEP THE SABBATH DAY HOLY

V. HONOR YOUR FATHER AND MOTHER

VI. DO NOT COMMIT MURDER

VII. DO NOT COMMIT ADULTERY

VIII. DO NOT STEAL

IX. DO NOT LIE

X. DO NOT COVET

THE FRUIT OF THE SPIRIT:
Galatians 5:22-23

LOVE

JOY

PEACE

PATIENCE

KINDNESS

GOODNESS

GENTLENESS

FAITHFULNESS

SELF-CONTROL

JESUS LOVES ME

Jesus loves me this I know
For the Bible tells me so
Little ones to Him belong
They are weak,
but He is strong

Yes, Jesus loves me
Yes, Jesus loves me
Yes, Jesus loves me
The Bible tells me so

Jesus take this heart of mine
Make it pure and holy thine
On the cross you died for me
I will try to live for thee

Yes, Jesus loves me
Yes, Jesus loves me
Yes, Jesus loves me
The Bible tells me so

*Jesus Loves Me – Public Domain

SOME INTERESTING FACTS ABOUT THE HOLY BIBLE:

The Bible is made up of 66 books

The Bible is made up of TWO parts:
The Old Testament and The New Testament

The Old Testament has 39 Books

The New Testament has 27 Books

The Bible was written by 35 -40 different authors
Over the course of thousands of years

There are over 351 Old Testament Prophecies Fulfilled in Jesus Christ

The first Book of the Bible is Genesis and the Last Book of the Bible is Revelation

ABOUT THE AUTHOR

Karen Michele Fitzpatrick grew up in Upstate New York with her mother, father, two brothers and her sister. After receiving her Bachelor's degree, Karen started a Master's degree in Music Therapy at New York University after meeting her husband and starting a family. While raising four children and developing educational programs for children, God called Karen into the pastoral ministry in 2001 where she began to serve in the Body of Christ in various capacities. Karen completed her ministerial credentials and divinity education in 2012/13 and became a licensed pastor and minister.

In 2017, the Lord directed Karen to begin work on developing a ministry to help the Body of Christ train up young leaders and support families in conflict and at risk. In September 2018, NOW Ministries, Inc. was born where Karen continues to develop programs for young lives and families and to teach, preach and proclaim the gospel of Jesus Christ to the nations.

Made in United States
Orlando, FL
25 April 2023